Frontier Parish

Frontier Parish

An Account of the Society for the Propagation of the
Gospel and the Anglican Church in America, Drawn
from the Records of the Bishop of London

Carson I. A. Ritchie

Rutherford • Madison • Teaneck
Fairleigh Dickinson University Press
London: Associated University Presses

Associated University Presses, Inc.
Cranbury, New Jersey 08512

Associated University Presses
108 New Bond Street
London W1Y OQX, England

Library of Congress Cataloging in Publication Data
Ritchie, Carson I.   A
Frontier parish.
Bibliography: p.
Includes index.
1. Church of England in America —   History
Sources. 2. Society for the Propagation of the Gospel
in Foreign Parts, London—History—Sources. 3. Missions
—United States—History—Sources. I. Title.
BX5881.R57   266'.3'73   75-3564
ISBN 0-8386-1735-2

PRINTED IN THE UNITED STATES OF AMERICA

for Eugenia

Contents

Preface

No papers ever demanded less introduction than the letters
that follow, letters written to the Bishop of London by the
missionaries of the Society for the Propagation of the Gospel and others from about 1690 to 1776, for here, if any-
where in colonial history, we have documents that speak for
themselves. As they speak we hear the voice of an epoch, not
perhaps that "united voice of America" which a patriot
refers to below, but certainly one of those still, small voices
which too often go unheard when they could do most good,
only afterwards to be remembered—the voice of one of the
consciences of America.

Many books have been written about the colonial American churches, and this is as it should be, for they form one of
the most interesting sides of a most interesting epoch. But
no one, so far as I am aware, has ever written a book solely
concerned with the missionaries' letters to the Bishop. Some
American compilers have, of course, dipped into the collection and left their marks upon it—ink marks—but I have
tried to avoid anything that might have appeared

elsewhere, so far as possible. I think it not unfair to describe the bulk of this book as being based on unpublished material. I hope that some of the discoveries I have made may be as new to my readers as they were to me: that there was a civil war raging in South Carolina during the colonial period; that the Bishop of London employed a pirate ship as his letter carrier; and that parishioners occasionally sent their ministers challenges to a duel.

The first problem that arises in dealing with a large unpublished collection of this sort is one of selection. How could I decide to choose, in the end, such a small collection of letters or parts of letters, ignoring one state entirely? My principle was to put before the reader only what would seem to be immediately interesting to him, even if he were not primarily interested in ecclesiastical history. For this reason, much of the fascinating material dealing with purely ecclesiastical matters has been withheld, and I have no doubt that some will complain that this book is all about churchmen and not about their church. As always, some of the best letters seem to have got left out, but perhaps this is a good thing, for they put up so many hares to be chased that a book many times this size could hardly have recorded the hunt. Whenever possible I have tried to give the complete letter of a writer, from a deep-seated conviction that letter-writing in colonial America possessed qualities denied to other periods and other lands, that the American letters of the time have a profound importance, not only for the history of the time, but for the history of the letter as an art. This conviction is a purely personal one, and I do not expect anyone else to share it without proof offered.

I mentioned earlier that these letters represent a voice of conscience. If that conscience was sometimes a bad one, it was not the missionaries' fault. They, and the whole of the church they represented, were caught in a chain of evil cause and effect, like the curse of Lancaster in Shakes-speare's historical plays. Like that curse, this one, too, was to be expunged by the battlefields of a civil war, but before it was, we are presented with the picture of men forced to act rightly in a wrong situation. It is this harrowing position that makes the story of the Anglican Church in America such a splendid, melancholy theme. How I wish it could have found a historian more worthy of it!

Acknowledgments

I should like to thank the Archbishop of Canterbury and the Trustees of the Lambeth Palace Library for permission to make use of the material contained in this book.

1

The Sea Adventure

A MONG the notable achievements of the British colonists in North America, one that is not the least remarkable has passed almost unnoticed—their possession of
what appears to have been the largest diocese in the world.
The word *appear* is used advisedly here, for the Americans
were not sure whether in fact they were the diocesans of the
Bishop of London, and the good prelate was even more
unsure whether he were their spiritual ruler. Nobody has
ever cleared up this question, vital though it is for an understanding of American church history.

In the reign of James I the then Bishop of London, Dr.
John King, had shown what his successors probably felt to
be an excess of zeal and had interested himself deeply in the
affairs of the "plantations" that were being set up in Virginia. His appointment as Member of the Council for Virginia began a bond between the two countries that was to be

severed only when certain members of the Scottish episcopacy, among the very last churchmen to remain loyal to the dynasty that Compton had served, met in a back room in Aberdeen and consecrated Bishop Seabury as the first American bishop. During the time between these two events, the faithful Anglicans of the new countries looked to Fulham Palace, London, where the Bishop lived, as their ecclesiastical headquarters. It may seem strange to many that the English had not created a bishop for the new country they had wrested from the Indians, or that the direction of its church should not have been confided to the head of the church, under Christ, under King James—to the Archbishop of Canterbury, that is. There was, however, a certain amount of that wild logic which is so characteristic of English church history in the situation. The Bishop of London was "ordinary" or spiritual governor of the ships in the Thames; consequently, by a sort of extension, he was assumed to be the governor of the colonists who had embarked in them. Already he had sent overseas the second American clergyman, Richard Bucke.[1] During a large part of the most flourishing time of the early Stuart colonization of America, the Archbishop of the day, George Abbot, was unable to assert his right to the spiritual domination of America had he wished to do so, because he had shot his gamekeeper with a crossbow, and although his position saved him from a trial for murder, his official functions were nevertheless curtailed.[2]

The complexity of the Bishop's position as regards America was hardly lessened by an enquiry instituted by Bishop Compton in 1675 into what he regarded as a possi-

---

1. William Warren Sweet, *The Story of Religions in America* (New York and London: Harper Bros., 1930), p. 40.
2. C.F. Pascoe, *Two Hundred Years of the S.P.G., 1701-1900*. An Historical account the Society, Based on a digest of the Society's Records (London: n.p., 1901), p. 2.

ble source of his authority over America—an order of the council "said to have been made to commit unto the Bishop of London for the time being the care and pastoral charge of sending over ministers into our British foreign plantations and having the jurisdiction of them."[3] There seems to have been a certain haze over the Jamesian plans for a bishop for America, but Archbishop Laud, a man of really soaring ambition, had formed a commission for the regulation of the spiritual affairs of the colonies and planned to send a bishop to administer to William Brewster's flock in New England. He was not content to have pushed one section of the Anglo-Saxon race into rebellion; America must follow suit. When the English civil war was over, Dr. Alexander Murray, a clerical cavalier who had shared the King's exile, was nominated as Bishop of Virginia, with a care of the American plantations generally, but nothing came of this nomination. Murray put down his enforced inactivity to the machinations of the "Cabal" ministry, but Archbishop Secker, going through the papers dealing with the appointment a hundred years later, felt that this was an incorrect view and that it was the motion to base the bishop's revenue on the revenue from the customs that frustrated the scheme.

As will be seen, the existence of a bishop on one side of the Atlantic and his flock on the other hardly tended to foster the infant church. There were continual suggestions that a bishop should be appointed for America, but nothing was done. This unhappy situation did not fail to arouse adverse comments from the Southern archbishops, but they were not very loud ones. So Erastian had the Church of England become that there was no one who would take the risk of

---

3. Dictionary of National Biography, ed. Sir Leslie Stephens, George Smith, s.v. Abbott (London: 1885).

offending the government, even to secure full religious rights for the American colonists. Secker, it is true, wrote

> I believe there scarce is or ever was, a Bishop of the Church of England from the Revolution to this day, that hath not desired the establishment of Bishops in our Colonies. Archbishop Tenison, who was surely no High Churchman, left by his will £1000 towards it. And many more, of the greatest eminence might be named, who were and are zealous for it.... Or if Bishops as such must of course be deemed partial, the Society for Propagating the Gospel consists partly also of inferior clergymen, partly too of laymen. Now the last cannot so well be suspected of designing to advance ecclesiastical authority. Yet this whole body of men, almost ever since it was in being, hath been making repeated application for Bishops in America; nor have the lay part of it ever refused to concur in them.[4]

He did not, however, dare to publish revolutionary sentiments in his lifetime and the letter was printed posthumously. Actions that we commit in spite of our consciences have a habit of bringing their rewards in this world as well as the next. The refusal of the British ministers to send out bishops to confirm the young, comfort the sinner, ordain ministers, and see that the clergy did their duty was to contribute in no small degree to the disintegration of the first British Empire in 1776.

Yet, the Americans were not quite without a bishop. They had the Bishop of London. He it was who performed for America most of her episcopal duties. He ordained clergymen, and exercised ecclesiastical discipline over them; he confirmed candidates for communion. If he were not America's bishop, then who was? We must remember that there can be dioceses without bishops, and perhaps if we think of America as a diocese, undivided as yet, adminis-

---

4. Arthur L. Cross, *The Anglican Episcopate and the American Colonies* (New York: Green and Co., 1902).

tered by the Bishop of London, but to which a suffragan bishop would be appointed some day, we would be nearest the truth. What a magnificent diocese it was! It included not only the American seaboard colonies, but the islands of the Caribbean and the Atlantic. The wide arc of the British possessions swept from Port of Spain to Halifax, and was later to extend to include Canada, running from the equator to the Arctic Circle. Yet, on this grand stage, the hero, that is, the bishop, was never to appear during British times. To continue the simile, the Anglican church in America was trying to play Hamlet without the Prince of Denmark. Their Hamlet was in Fulham Palace. There were not wanting those who drew the correct inference from the one essential ingredient of an Episcopal church and murmured, "It will not, nor it cannot come to good." Contemporaries felt that it was not only a unique diocese but a unique situation, a flock with their bishop three thousand miles away. Secker, whose upbringing as a Presbyterian had broadened his outlook somewhat, admitted that it was a state of affairs "without parallel in the Christian world."[5] The Archbishop was not strong on history, or he would have recollected that the Roman Catholic Primate of Great Britain at the end of the previous century, Vicar Apostolic John Leyburn, Bishop of Adramite, was spiritual leader not only of the English Catholics, but of those in all the English colonies in America as well.[6] There was a good deal of justification for this in his case, however, for the number of Catholics in America did not warrant a separate bishop's establishment.

The Virginia church foreshadowed, in many ways, the

5. Quoted in Andrew G. Drummond, *The Story of American Protestantism* (Edinburgh: Oliver and Boyd, 1949).
6. See Carson I.A. Ritchie, "Papers From Lambeth Palace Library," Catholic Record Society, Miscellanea (London, 1964), for an account of Leyburn.

troubles that were to beset the Anglicans in America as a whole. It was completely under the control of the state. The personal character of the royal governor influenced the condition of the clergy; thus we are told that under the rule of Governor John Harvey the characters of the ministers sent out to the colony underwent a change for the worse.[7] The fact that the laws for the church were made by the General Assembly often meant that the church was being administered by the state purely in secular interests. The appointment of ministers in each parish was in the hands of a vestry, which was empowered, after 1661, to fill its own vacancies, and the removal of a minister could be obtained on complaint of the vestry to the governor and his council. This often meant that a minister might be turned out as soon as he had exhausted his stock of sermons and had ceased to be novelty to his parish. The clergy were paid their salaries in leaf tobacco, sixteen thousand pounds a year. Since the price of tobacco dropped steadily throughout the eighteenth century, this meant that the clergy were growing progressively impoverished as the period wore on. The condition of the glebe, the arable land that was supposed to contribute to the clergy's support, was often very unsatisfactory.[8] Without a cat to watch them, the mice began to play. Anglican ministers at home had never been left without the supervision of a commissary or official, the ecclesiastical officials whose duty it was to discipline the clergy and see that they obeyed the ecclesiastical laws. When, therefore, they found themselves in America where there was little possibility of being brought to account for their misdeeds it is not surprising that the strict behavior that was expected of a minister of the Gospel slackened somewhat.

People of the time did not take this view; they felt that the

7. Sweet, p. 53.
8. *Ibid.*

government at home was getting rid of the least promising of the English clergy by sending them to the colonies. "Of all commodities, so of this," wrote their Governor. "The worst are sent us." A Virginia rector wrote to the Bishop telling him that scandalous clergymen had so disgusted the laity that they could with difficulty be persuaded to take a clergyman into their house.[9] It is a little unfair to the Bishop of London to suggest that he deliberately got rid of his worst clergy by sending them to Virginia. No doubt clergymen who were well known as bad characters might find it convenient to take a trip to the colonies, but the reason for the complaints against the Virginia clergy lies in the failure of the Bishop to control them properly. It is only necessary to read through the pages of the records of an ordinary whose duty it was to discipline the clergy, such as the Official of the Archdeacon of St. Albans, in England about this time, to see how difficult it was to keep the English clergy in control, even with the aid of what was a reasonably well-functioning system of ecclesiastical correction. The Archdeaconry comprised only twenty-four parishes, so there were never more than twenty-four ministers in it at the one time. Even with this small number of clerics, it was very seldom that the Official was not obliged to take action of some sort against an offending parson. During the sixteenth and seventeenth centuries their parishioners accused them of all sorts of crimes; they had quarreled violently with their flock, and knocked some of them down with their fists; they had neglected their duties regarding sermons and burials, preached false doctrine, and insulted their congregation in church. They had got drunk; debauched their parishioners' wives, had bastards by their maid-servants and buried them in pails in the parsonage yard. If the Elizabethan and

9. *Ibid*, p. 55.

Jamesian clergy behaved like this at home, under the supervision of the system of church courts that controlled them, it was not to be expected that they would behave better abroad, uncontrolled.[10]

The complaints that began to filter home led to the sending out, in 1685, of James Blair as the Bishop's Commissary to correct ecclesiastical offenses. Blair held visitations, or examinations and trials of defaulting parsons, and did much to raise the morality and efficiency of the Virginia church. Meanwhile the Anglicans had been establishing themselves in Maryland, beginning with only three clergymen, about whom more will be said later. The succeeding Anglican clergymen here were considered by the historian Lodge to be even worse than those in Virginia.[11] So bad were they that a particularly brutal or dissolute parson was commonly known in the colonies as "a Maryland parson."[12] Dr. Thomas Bray, a Warwickshire clergyman, was sent out as Commissary in 1696 to reform the church there. He acted firmly and energetically, and did much for the intellectual as well as the moral life of the colony. Unfortunately, he quarreled with the testy Scots Governor, Francis Nicolson, who, as we shall see, was annoyed at being "kicked upstairs" into Maryland after holding office in Virginia, and also with the clergy, on whom he attempted to impose the Anglican Prayer Book. Criticisms of his actions in Parliament led to his return, and the chief result of his visit was to be the institution of two missionary societies in England, the Society for Promoting Christian Knowledge and the Society for the Propagation of the Gospel.[13]

10. Archdeaconry of St. Albans (hereafter A.S.A.) records, Hertford County Record Office, Hertford, England.
11. Quoted in Drummond, p. 15.
12. Henry K. Rowe, *The History of Religion in the United States* (New York: Macmillan & Co., 1924), p. 15.
13. Drummond, p. 16.

Plans for the constitution of the former society were laid before the Bishop in 1697, and the first meeting of the S.P.C.K., as it came to be called, was held in 1695. During the interval that elapsed while Bray sailed for Maryland, a committee of twelve was named in Convocation "to enquire into ways and means for promoting Christian religion in our Foreign Plantations." Bray, on his return to England, appealed to William III for his help, and at a meeting of the society in May 1701 a draft of the charter for erecting a corporation "for propagating the Gospel in Foreign Parts" was read, and the society came into being. Letters patent were granted to it under the Great Seal, and the first meeting of the Society for the Propagation of the Gospel in Foreign Parts was held on June 27, 1701, in Lambeth Palace. The gathering consisted of one of the archbishops, four bishops, four knights, a dean, two archdeacons, seven reverend doctors, two doctors, and a leaven of nine untitled laymen. It was a distinguished enough company no doubt, but hardly consisting of "the noblest in the land," as one historian has described it, seeing that it numbered so many parsons. Indeed, one of the essential characteristics of the eighteenth-century parson is his social inferiority. He was not, in most companies, considered good enough to remain at table with his betters while the more special part of the meal—the dessert—made its appearance, so he usually disappeared when the pudding was brought in. At the following meeting the design for the society's seal was chosen, that of "a ship under sail, making towards a point of land, upon the prow standing a minister with an open bible in his hand, people standing on the shore in a posture of expectation."[14]

14. C.F. Pascoe, *Two Hundred Years of the S.P.G., 1701-1900*. An Historical account of the Society, Based on a digest of the Society's Records (London: n.p., 1901), p. 6. The Society's Seal was copied from that of Massachusetts Bay, insofar as the motto went, which was, in the Massachusetts seal "Come over and help us," and in the Society's "Transiens adiua nos," the same thing in a different language.

Well might the American congregations so stand, but whether they expected all they were to get I shall leave to the reader to decide for himself.

Before setting out for the colonies, the missionaries provided by the Society were ordered to call on the Archbishop of Canterbury for instructions. On board ship they were to conduct themselves so as to be examples of piety and virtue to the ship's company; they were to try to prevail upon the captain to have morning and evening prayer and special services on Sunday. On their arrival in the country where they were sent, they were to "be circumspect, not board or lodge in public houses, game (that is, gamble) not at all, converse not with lewd persons, save to admonish them; be frugal, keep out of debt, not meddle with politics, keep away from quarrels, say the service every day, when practicable, and always with seriousness and decency; avoid high flown sermons, preach against such vices as they see to prevail, impress the nature and need of the sacraments, distribute the society's tracts and visit their people." The salary of the missionaries was to be fifty pounds a year, besides ten pounds for their outfit.[15]

These provisions were perhaps better fitted for the meridian in which they were composed—that of St. Martins in the Fields, London, than for the Atlantic seaboard. In a part of the world where so much of the labor was convict, where the local politicians might be highwaymen in exile, and where every second person had either done something discreditable or was supposed to have done so before coming out, how was the missionary to avoid "lewd company"? How was he to keep free from debt when prices were so much greater than at home, and where he might be met at the boat by the governor, who then borrowed his salary for the year and forgot to pay it back?

15. Sweet, p. 242.

The launching of the first wave of missionaries on the American continent virtually settled the form that Anglicanism was to take on that continent: "the history of the Church of America is to be looked for in the records of the Venerable Society." It is, I submit, because so much of these records, in particular those letters which will be quoted below, have remained generally unknown, that false notions about American Anglicanism have been put forward, even by competent historians. To give only one example of this tendency, it is often said that sects other than the Anglican were hostile to the idea of an American bishop. How wrong this is will, it is hoped, appear in the following pages.

It will not always be convenient or indeed necessary to distinguish below between those parsons mentioned in the letters who were missionaries and those who had come to the colonies of their own accord and subsequently obtained the Bishop's license to officiate in America. Both kinds of clergymen corresponded freely with the Bishop, their purpose in so doing being made plain by the kinds of letters they wrote. Not only clergymen, but governors, parishioners, church wardens, laymen, and Mr. Anonymous wrote as well. In general, it was to a desire to obtain the Bishop's advice or concurrence that we owe the collection of letters from which the extracts and examples that compose so great a part of this book are drawn. It is not difficult to imagine the bishop sitting in his palace in Fulham and opening these letters and reading them. There is no doubt that he did read most of his correspondence, ponder on it, and go as far as to make, or have made, a summary note of the contents on the back. These notes are usually short, and always uninformative. When some writer has been tearing out his heartstrings describing to the Bishop a state of affairs in the Maryland Church that must surely bring down a judgment on the state in general, the prelate will merely note on the back "bad cl'men [clergymen] Maryland." Occasionally the Bishop acted promptly on the receipt of a letter, sometimes he wrote back in reply, but on occasion he did not trouble to do so, and the correspondent who had addressed him was obliged, in his next communication, to make use of some system of reference, such as to allude to "the second letter I sent you after the one to which you replied." Often these unanswered letters were from ministers or persons of no importance, poor devils of missionaries to whom it would not be seemly for his lordship to condescend by replying, but occasionally they were from people of such status (one of his commissaries for example) and on topics of an importance that would have seemed to have merited an immediate reply. The reader, then, need not feel that he is reading an unduly one-sided correspondence, as the pattern of these letters unfolds, or is missing a great deal without the Bishop's replies before him. He may be pardoned, too, if he comes to the conclusion that to the Bishop of London, America seemed far away and sometimes a little unreal.

"Religion," wrote a poetaster of the time, "religion stands a tip toe on our strand,/Waiting to pass to the American land." Between the missionaries and their goal lay three thousand miles of angry water and a crossing with a bad reputation. Strangely enough, it was not of the dangers that the parsons thought, as they collected their belongings before boarding one of the tobacco ships that spread their white wings in the English seaports every spring, but of the difficulties of leaving England at all. Some of them were so convinced of the difficulties that it was a difficult business to get them to leave. "That I may not incur your Lordship's displeasure by staying so long in England," wrote a missionary "I beg leave to lay before your Lordship the reasons of it. I have, may it please your Lordship, been much afflicted of late with a tedious ague and feaver, and thereby an expence has ensued beyond what I am able to bear. This I say to your Lordship, though I would not have the world acquainted with it, but I assure your Lordship that without assistance I can't pretend to equip myself for the voyage."[16] Even the journey to the port of embarkation for America might be no inconsiderable feat. Robert Jenney, writing from the north of Ireland, told the Bishop: "I shall take the opportunity of the spring ships to make my voyage to America, and in order thereto set out from hence three weeks hence, or perhaps sooner."[17] Readers of Swift will remember the difficulties that faced Jenney: the coach to Cork, then a storm-crossed voyage to Holyhead, high-waymen, floods, bad roads, no one but Welshmen to talk to, coaches again through Chester to London.

Once the archiepiscopal blessing had been obtained, parsons had a choice of two ways of making the voyage: in a ship of the Merchant Service, or aboard one of His Majesty's warships. Most people, given the choice, would have chosen the latter. It was slower, it was much more uncomfortable, but it was likely to be safer, for the risk of capture at sea by the French was considerable.

Clergymen were not regarded as noncombatants in the eighteenth century. The second Bishop of Quebec, captured in the Seine, by British cruisers, spent years in a British prison. Le Loutre, the apostle of the Micmacs, and the principal center for Acadian resistance to the British in Halifax, was captured crossing the Atlantic and kept in detention for a long time. Fortunately for himself, he was able to conceal his identity; if his captors had suspected

16. Fulham Papers, 9/218. 25th June 1716, Evan Evans to the Bishop of London (hereafter B of L), "The memorial of John Evans."
17. *Ibid.*, 14th Jan., 1745, Robert Jenney to the Bishop of London, "Harrymount near Lurgan in the north of Ireland."

whom they held, they would certainly have hanged him, in spite of convention. Twenty-four Catholic missals intended for the diocese of Quebec, just as they came from the Paris booksellers, remain in Lambeth Palace Library as a silent monument to this mutual capture of churchmen; they had been in the possession of the ill-fated St. Vallier when his ship was captured. It seems a pity that some of them, at least, can not continue their voyage to the church for which they were intended. Clergymen were, in fact, looked on by enemy governments, not as servants of the Prince of Peace, but as paid uniformed officials of a hostile state. They seem to have determined to capture as many of each others churchmen as possible, and to treat them as badly as they could.

> Les Anglais font des prisonniers,
> Nous en faisons des milliers,
> Voilà le ressemblance.
> Le Français les traite bien,
> Mais l'Anglais les traite en chien,
> Voilà le différence.[18]

Consequently, a missionary crossing the Atlantic perhaps risked more than other folk. The sort of things that could happen to a clergyman making an Atlantic voyage can seen from the sad stories of the Reverend Messrs. Heskith and Cordiner. Heskith had been captured, as so many American voyagers were, by the privateers of Dunkirk. These daring seamen, venturing into the Channel approaches in small craft, took a regular toll of the rich British merchant ships that beat past their harbors. Heskith describes the experience of falling into their hands laconically: "After some dispute we were boarded and taken. I shan't trouble my reader here with a detail of their usage, only observe this

18. French Canadian marching song of the time.

much, that anyone who unhappily falls into their hands may look upon it as an act of grace if they are not stripped naked."[19] Clothes were, of course, worth money in these days, and were worth having, hence the eighteenth-century habit of stripping prisoners. Heskith was thrown into the common jail at Dunkirk, only to be transferred a few hours later to the *Conciergerie*, "a place for officers who are prisoners of war to eat and sleep in." He now had freedom to move about the town, accompanied by a sentry, and enjoyed this partial liberty for three months. Then, to follow Heskith's own account, "this small glimmering of happiness was totally eclipsed by the malicious suggestions and restless endeavours of the British and Irish priests in Dunkirque." Dunkirk and the other privateer towns were full of British Jacobites; many of the letters of marque—the privateer's commission to make war—were issued to people with Irish or Scotch names, such as Dunbar, Fitzgerald, Lambert, and Geraldine. The Jacobite garrisoning of the Bass Rock off the British coast, one of the most remarkable feats of arms of the period, was being fed by the Dunkirk luggers, in the teeth of the British navy. Hence all the bitterness of civil war. The parson had had many disputations with those priests who had come to visit him, and he had also done his best to stop them from enlisting recruits from among the English prisoners in Dunkirk in the Irish regiments in French service, "particularly in that commanded by the young Lord Clare [the famous 'Clare's Dragoons'] then at St. Omers." His arguments on behalf of Anglicanism, and against enlistment in the French army, according to Heskith's account "coming to the ear of my Lady Abbess and one Creighton, Father Confessor to the Nunnery, they resolved to endeavour my close confinement, and for that

19. A narrative of Mr. Heskith's imprisonment (Lambeth Palace, London; hereafter L.P.L.).

end they petitioned the Intendant of Marines that I might be clapped into prison as one who disputed against the religion of the government, and which was more, the only true religion in the world." The Intendant replied that since Heskith was an English prisoner of war, he could not be put into solitary confinement simply for officiating as a clergyman. The Bishop of Quebec,[20] however, had been captured recently, and one of his chaplains, "the Sieur de Sonjon, was by no means treated in England, either as suitably to his character or as a prisoner of war." The Intendant therefore proposed that punitive measures should be instituted against him as a reprisal for the supposed ill treatment of the chaplain. The French government was acting here with considerable ambivalence, for they were heartily glad that the Bishop was in custody. Though a man of saintly fervor of character, he had succeeded in offending all the very sectional interests in Quebec, and the British were doing Louis XIV a favor by keeping him a prisoner. It was, then, a little intransigent to complain about the treatment of one of a party of clerics who could have been exchanged without too much trouble, if only France were willing. Any stick was good enough for the French authorities to beat a clerical prisoner with, however, and as Heskith writes "I was committed close prisoner to the common jail, upon the 20th of August old stile, 1707, and remained there in durance for thirty days; for in that time the Commissaries had acquainted the Intendant (by a letter from Mr. Lyn their secretary) that the Sieur Desonjon was at liberty and well treated, and therefore on that account they expected that I should be immediately released, upon the receipt of which letter, the Intendant ordered me to be set at liberty wisely

20. Jean Baptiste de la Croix Chevrière de St. Vallier (1653-1727), Bishop of Quebec, spent nineteen years in detention. He was kept in Paris from 1694 to 1697 and again from 1709 to 1713. In between times he was a prisoner in England.

concluding that if I was not, there was just reason to fear that some of their ecclesiastics (in England) might be made reprisals." The two governments had set out to race each other in their ill treatment of clerical prisoners, with the most unfortunate consequences for the outgoing missionaries.

Heskith returned to his old, comfortable lodgings, only to find them taken up by some British officers who had just been captured on the brig *Nightingale*. He moved elsewhere and settled down to the pleasant, rather vague half life of the prisoner on parole. As he sipped his wine in the auberges and exchanged news with the other British and American merchant marine officers, he probably thought that his troubles were over. In reality, they had just begun. An order now came through that all English officers were to move from Dunkirk to Calais. Moving their prisoners about pointlessly was one of the amusements of the French bureaucrats of the time, probably because they could extort money from them for their journeying expenses. Heskith was forced to go to Calais, and from there still further, to Amiens. The prevost told him that he would get him a good horse for the journey, but that it would cost him 3/6d. a day. Heskith objected in vain to this depletion of his slender resources. He was lucky to have money to stop the mouths of the French officials; the fate of those prisoners who did not possess any was, as the reader will see shortly, not a pleasant one. Heskith was welcomed at Amiens by the local official, who found him quarters, first at an inn, which he left because he found he had to eat at irregular hours, and then in private lodgings, which proved more suitable. On the seventh of March, however, the dreadful news reached him that orders had arrived from the French Court, signed by Jerome Phorlypaux de Pontchartrain, Secretary of State for Maritime Affairs, and directed to the Intendant of

Picardy, which ordered him to put the clergyman in irons and throw him into the *cachot*. He was to be used as "reprisal" for Captain Smith and "one Nally, (alias Campbell) an Irish priest, who were taken in the Nightingale by Captain Haddock, and who were both at that time in irons in Newgate." It will be remembered that the parson had been unable to get back his old lodgings because they were occupied by prisoners taken by the French on board the British ship *Nightingale*. This sloop had been captured in September 1707 during a raid on the English coast by Thomas Smith, a former English naval officer. This gentleman, who was presumably a Jacobite, had sold the ship he commanded in the British navy, *Bonetta*, to Sweden, and enlisted with the French privateers. Although quite justified in what he had done, according to his principles, his activities had made him so obnoxious to the British that the captain of *Nightingale* (the same man who was presumably now sleeping in Heskith's old bed) treacherously tried to run him through after surrendering to him. Smith had made another raid on the English coast in the *Nightingale*, now renamed *Rossignol*, but had been captured. He and the Irish priest, Nally, who had come with him (presumably on Jacobite secret-service activity) were now chained up in Newgate. Heskith was thrown into the *cachot*, the general dungeon of the prison, an institution that, overlooked by the march of progress, differed little from that in which St. Paul had spent so much of his ministry. We leave poor Heskith then, chained to the wall, and probably in total darkness and some inches of water, to take up the adventures of another intrepid minister.

Mr. William Cordiner was a living exposition of the theme that will, I hope, find further development in this book, that of the bravery to be found in perfectly ordinary men and women when a situation arises that calls it forth.

Such calls were not wanting in the American colonial period, nor did they go unanswered, which is one of the reasons why it has such an attraction for the student. Not many people, in choosing to tell a story of stark heroism, would select a curate as a hero, but Cordiner, before he became a minister of the Amercian Church, was a curate at Billyaghran, in Ireland. Early in 1707, Cordiner, who was then about twenty-seven, was selected as a missionary to go out to Shrewsbury parish in Cecil County, Maryland. He decided to take out with him his entire family, in the eighteenth-century sense of the word—that is, his wife, his old mother, two children, and servant. Not unnaturally Cordiner wanted to make a safe passage, so he approached the Admiralty, and got a passage on *Dover*, a man-of-war which, however, became disabled and had to stay in port. Cordiner accordingly embarked with his party in *Chester*, another warship sailing for America. He had thought of sailing in *Ruby*, another Queen's ship in the convoy, but the captain "told me I should have very bad conveniencies if I went with him, for they were very much crowded, having the Governor of Virginia and others aboard of him."[21] He therefore got an order from the Admiralty to the Chester's captain, Balchen, no doubt congratulating himself on having secured the prosperity of the voyage.

It was unfortunate for the Cordiners that at this moment the private navy of the privateer admiral, Duguay Trouin, was sweeping the trade routes in the Atlantic. Trouin was associated in this venture with the regular naval staff officer, Claude Comte de Fourbin, formerly admiral of the Siamese navy, very unfortunately for Trouin, for his colleague was one of those officers who would rather lose any battle according to the book of rules than abandon them by

21. "An Abstract of Mr. Cordiner's Journal" (L.P.L., MS. 937). This is a shortened version of the original journal, which is in the S.P.G. records.

doing something original. More than outbalancing the count's formalism, however, was the quality of the privateer officers and crews that Trouin had under his command. At least as efficient as the best English privateers in their best period, that is, under Drake, they were spurred on by a nice system of incentives. Whereas for the English navymen victory meant flogging and harsh treatment, with a sprinkling of prize money if the Admiralty could be persuaded to pay up, every privateer knew that he fought for his own interests and that a lucky hit might enable him to retire in comfort. Not surprisingly, the privateers never hesitated to engage British forces of twice their strength, and frequently showed them that Bretons never never never will be slaves.

On the morning of Friday October 9, Trouin's private navy sighted the Virginia Fleet, and after an interchange with Fourbin that drew forth the famous retort from the privateer "My duty to my King overrides that to my Admiral!" Trouin sailed in to attack them, leaving Fourbin observing behind him. What followed can best be described in Cordiner's own words. "They came up with us and engaged us; in two hours' time the *Cumberland, Chester* and *Ruby* were taken, the *Devonshire* burned, and the *Royal Oak* made the best of her way for Ireland. Our engagement was sharp; we had thirty seven men on our quarter deck who were all killed and wounded excepting Captain Balchen, our Commander, the master, and a boy. As soon as they boarded us they came down to the Cockpit where my family was, and searched all of us to the skin, and took all that we had from us. The sailors took compassion of the women and children, and threw them some things again, which the chief officers took from them and stripped them three several times. Nay, they took the very shoes and stockings from my little children. My loss here was very great, to the value of two hundred pounds and upwards." We now leave the Cordiner family to look once more at Parson Heskith.

This cleric, who seems to have been a hard man to intimidate, was in a state of extreme indignation, not so much at being chained up as at being used as a cat's-paw by the French for the second time to obtain better treatment for their Jacobite agents, and at being confined in a jail along with murderers and thieves. "When I saw myself," he writes, "put into the same predicament with those criminals, who were doomed by their laws to the rack, to the wheel or to the galleys, this filled my mind with a just abhorrency of their illegal proceedings and with all the passions of a due resentment." He wrote to the Intendant, pointing out that both Captain Smith and Nally were subjects of Queen Anne, and that therefore he ought not to be used a "reprisal" for them, "because one subject can't be made a reprisal for another." The Intendant remarked that Heskith's reasoning was "bold and impertinent." Smith and Nally were subjects of King James, not of the present "surreptitious government." "Consequently I was a just reprisal; and might be well assured that whatever punishment they [Smith and Nally] suffered in England, I'd reason to expect the same treatment here in France." The English and French governments were playing off their clerical hostages against one another, a form of barter not warranted by their status as prisoners of war. No one was going to worry about points of international law such as that, however. This fact was further rubbed home by a threatening letter Heskith now received from Father Patrick Touel (Toole?), chaplain and confessor to the Comte de Fourbin. The Count had just botched one of the few really promising bids to restore the Stuarts to the throne of England by refusing to land James III and his party in Scotland, on the ground that, because the English admiral Byng was following them, it was innoportune. Better at ill-treating prisoners than capturing them himself, he was using his chaplain as an English amanuensis to insist that Heskith must get Nally released if he valued his own life. The poor parson now realized for the first time that he might be shortly wearing something more constrictive than a clerical cravat, and he wrote home desperately to his friends in England, urging them to get the Jacobites released at all costs. At length he succeeded, but the lawyers determined to play out their solemn farces to the end, and it was not until the formality of a *Nolle prosequi* was entered into that Nally was released from Newgate and Heskith's shackles struck off. The clergyman's journal, which has remained unpublished, solves the centuries' old problem of why Nally escaped the death penalty that poor Smith suffered. "[Aslaby and Father Nally]n" says a recent writer,[22] "were by some influence now unknown, acquitted and exchanged!"

So much for Mr. Heskith; now free, he hastened back to England. Meanwhile we take up the Cordiner story where it left off. There is a heavy sea running, the stiff wind cracks out the Fleur de Lys flying above the White Ensign, and water seeps in through the holes shot in the *Chester's* sides. What the Americans in the Cockpit, their friends in London, and their relatives in the colonies feel like can best be imagined by recollecting the passage in the contemporary novel *Moll Flanders*, where someone says "The worst has happened," and another character replies, "What, is the Virginia Fleet taken?"

"They kept us aboard nine days rolling on the sea," says Cordiner, "without the allowance of either meat or drink, and but very little clothing, lying in a very pitiful and dismal condition. Sometimes their seamen or some of ours that spoke French brought us a little bread and cheese and some water. "They made Brest on October 19 and Cordiner and his family stayed in the town for twelve days. During that

---

22. *W. Branch Johnson, Wolves of the Channel, 1681-1856* (London: Wishart & Co., 1931).

time the parson received one of the many kindnesses done to him by disinterested French civilians when two monks whose acquaintance he had made went with him to the Intendant General to petition on his behalf for horses to help carry his family to their eventual place of captivity. The little convoy of Americans and British sailors now began a march of death that was to cost the life of Cordiner's child, his servant, and many others.

At the first stage of the journey, Landerneau, the Intendant refused to allow the minister more than one horse to carry his family, of whom there were, of course, seven, in spite of the promise the official in Brest had made that there would be horses for all. "What to do then," says Cordiner, "I could not tell, for he threatened to beat me if I said any more. I got some of our men that spoke French to desire them to be patient and get me that one horse, which I had, and bought two panniards, putting a child in each, and set my mother between them, and my wife and I walked." The march east continued to Landirigian, Morlaix, le Pontu. Although Mrs. Cordiner was pregnant, her husband was unable to get a horse for her. "I was obliged to be up till eleven at night," he remarks, "and rise at three or four in the morning every day to get them [the two horses] in readiness, my servants being so wearied were not able to assist me. We had the allowance of 5d. a day for each, and I borrowed some money from our officers at Brest, which hired a horse to carry my wife. Our lodging was both bad and dear. We paid 3d. a night for each, even for the children, and provision was so dear we could afford ourselves very little." The convoy crawled on through St. Ambril to Languez, the sailor prisoners, and also probably those Americans who, unlike Cordiner, had been unable to borrow money, suffering very severely. "Several of our men," he writes, "were so wearied that the Prevosts were obliged to leave them there, having whipped them forwards so long as they were able to stand, nay until some have fallen to the ground and pissed blood." Probably as his slender stock of cash diminished, Cordiner's treatment from the prevosts got progressively worse. Certainly there came a day when they could no longer beat the minister and his wife into a stumbling walk. Then "the provosts threatened and abused us, and at length left us in that poor condition on the way, and took my mother and the children along with them. On the one hand I feared the boors [country people] would come and strip us, for they used to serve our men so that were left behind on the way, on the other, expecting to lie there all night, was afraid we might perish before morning, it being a very great frost. But God was merciful to us in this very strait, for we were not there half an hour before we saw a gentleman riding towards us, and hearing my wife weep so bitterly, he came and spoke to me in Latin. I told him my condition, upon which he rode after the prevosts and brought one of their horses back to carry my wife, and was very angry with them for treating us so barbarously." Glad to be alive, they got into Fugiers, where they stayed for a month. Fugiers was the stage to which the Intendant had originally promised Cordiner horses, but it will have been seen how he kept his word. At Fugiers the people were friendly, though very poor, and provisions were cheap.

When the order came for a move, this time to Dinan, another nightmare journey began. "I had the liberty of a cart to carry my family with the sick," Cordiner wrote. "We had a great many sick men carried in a very poor condition, and when they complained they had nothing but blows. It rained all the time we were on this journey, which cost several of our men their lives. Some of them dropping out of the carts have lain in the way until they perished."

At Dinan Cordiner was able to begin a regular ministry to

the civilian and military prisoners there, reading prayers every day and preaching twice on Sunday. Religious toleration of this sort reflects great credit on the French government. The Presbyterian Scots, although united politically to England at this time, found the sound of Anglican worship so offensive to their ears that the chaplains of English regiments stationed in Scotland were not permitted to conduct their accustomed services. A Father Hagan, who like many Irish priests in France was a recruiting agent for the Irish regiments in Louis XIV's service, gave orders to the sentry that he was not to be admitted to preach to the sailor prisoners in the castle, and Cordiner therefore confined his work thenceforth to the town, where about three hundred naval and merchant marine officers were kept under a sort of open arrest. Many of the latter were no doubt, like Cordiner, American civilians.

When he reaches this stage in the abstract of his journal, the parson stops to make a little calculation, and reckons that the party have now achieved a march of 230 miles. The distance was probably rather less, if, as he thought, they had marched 80 leagues; allowing for the variation of the French league, this would make the distance about 200 miles. "We brought from Fugiers to this town," he continues, "about 1000 men, and in a little were about 700. In four or five months we had two hundred died in a very pitiful case. I can't say but the King ordered a good allowance for prisoners, but this I must say, that they are greatly cheated in getting of it. There is a good hospital in Brest and our wounded men [were] carefully attended to there, but there is one in Dinan which is [a] place to dispatch men out of the world and not to prolong their life in it."

The French government had been hoping to regain its captured nationals by the simple process of taking over England under a Stuart King, but Fourbin had, as we have seen, nipped this hope in the bud. Rather illogically, the French blamed the Scots, cursing them bitterly and crying "Scot will be Scot still, always false."[23] The influence of the Scots and Irish Jacobites, which had done much to embitter the lot of American and English prisoners, was at once reduced to zero, and the French, having failed in their attempt to use force, had to fall back on negotiation. An exchange of prisoners took place through the machinery of the commissioners for prisoners who resided in each country. Transports sailed for England with three hundred of the privateer's captives aboard, the Cordiners among them, all except a child and one of the servants, who had died in prison. The minister was now ruined financially. Not only had he lost all his money when the ship was taken, but he had run up a lot of debts while in prison—prisoners at this time had, of course, to pay for their own support. The Society gave him money to pay his French creditors "who were kind to me and my family, during my imprisonment, and let me have money on my own bills." He was, however, still much impoverished.

The Cordiners, experiences do much to explain why people were so anxious to escape from poverty and hardship on one side of the Atlantic for what was often poverty and hardship on the other. Sufferers like the parson and his family must have felt with some reason that nothing worse could happen to them in their new home than what they had already experienced in the most civilized country of the Old World. An Iroquois war party would not have left prisoners behind alive to die miserably of exposure nor have killed them by the deprivation of food and decent treatment. The barbarity of the American savage erupted from his volcanic passions and therefore subsided when

23. Pascoe, p. 32.

those passions had died down, while the barbarity of Europe was on the statute book, and therefore eternal. The Indians burned some of their enemies at the stake because they wished to sacrifice them to the God of War; English law burned at the stake a man or woman servant who had killed his or her master because it wanted to make a world comfortable for employers to live in. Against this dark European background of invasion, civil war, and racial and religious hatred, the white sails of the ships carrying the missionaries to the colonies shone all the more brightly.

We have seen that the clerical voyager stood in rather greater danger than his lay counterpart at this time, and it was a danger that did not diminish. The condition of privateers' prisoners got worse rather than better throughout the century, as more privateers came into being in response to the increasing merchants that the British sent to sea. Anyone captured by the French at sea might consider himself lucky if he escaped with his life. Forty-nine years after the events described, a young Bedfordshire Nonconformist squire watched the dead bodies of thirty-one of his fellow prisoners at Dinan being thrown into a single trench. This experience turned him into the unlikely path of social reform and he embarked on a crusade to improve prison conditions all over the world.

No privilege, then, attached to the clerical cloth; rather the reverse. The clergy on both sides had taken to heart St. Paul's injunction to "live peaceably with all men inasmuch as it lieth in you" and, being realists, understood that in the conditions of frontier warfare "inasmuch as" meant "not at all." Father Rale was killed gallantly defending his mission against the New Englanders, and a young Harvard ordinand kept the score in Lovewell's Fight by scalping the Indians as they fell. Consequently, every cleric of one side whom the other could detain represented the loss of a potential fighter; more than that, every clergyman was worth several soldiers as a stimulant to morale.

The considerations that had made the curate of Ballyaghran choose a warship to cross the Atlantic in moved Robert Jenney, a missionary whom we encountered some pages back, to do the same. Besides being forbidden, like the naval chaplains of the day, the use of the quarter galleries or water closets, and forced to use the heads, he came under naval discipline from the first. "I hoped," he wrote, "to have the honour to wait upon your Lordship before we entered upon our voyage for New York, but Admiral Cavendish who commands here being provoked by the non attendance of a great number of chaplains of men of war, some of whom he hath ordered to be pricked run[24] hath absolutely refused me liberty to return to London."[25] Once a passage had been obtained on a merchant ship, on the other hand, it was difficult to change or delay the sailing date. "Upon my resolution to come over into America," remarked Richard Peters, "I applied to Mr. Edward Markland, a gentleman well known to your Lordship, to inform you of my design, and to procure for me your Lordship's licence and letters of recommendation, but unfortunately for me he was seized with the gout at St. Albans and by that means having taken a cabin and laid in accomodations and sea stores I was obliged to proceed without your Lordship's letter."[26]

The old belief that parsons were Jonahs who brought bad luck on the ships in which they sailed, which was widely held by sailors, seems to have received some justification from the amount of bad weather and other mishaps that the

---

24. That is, entered on the ship's books as a deserter. Robert Jenney, L.L.D., was a missionary at New York, 1715-16. He later moved to Hempsted, and became Commissary in Pennsylvania, and Rector of Christ Church, Philadelphia. Died 1762.
25. 9/118. His Majesty's Ship *Lanceston* at Portsmouth, August 7, 1742.
26. Fulham Papers; 9/147. Richard Peters, Philadelphia.

missionaries' ships encountered. This may have been the reason why the third missionary to go out, after a very rough passage down channel, was "cursed and treated very ill on board."[27] Whether, with so many Welshmen among the missionaries, Davy Jones was determined to have as many of his compatriots with him as might be, is difficult to say, but their losses at sea were very high. No doubt the figure Pascoe gives for the loss of life among returning American ordinands, one in five,[28] is comparable in this case. Poor Mr. Cordiner was nearly drowned in harbor. "Waiting at Spitehead a long time," he wrote, "for a fair wind, I went ashore to write to the Honourable Society and get some fresh provisions for my family, being to sail that day. But returning met with an accident, a hoy running our long boat aboard, heaved it all to pieces. Blessed be God it was calm weather, so that the hoy took us all safe up."[29] A ship wrecked clergyman wrote to the Bishop to tell him: "The great goodness and favour your Lordship has been pleased to show my brother emboldens me to implore your Lordship's compassion in my distress. After a long and dangerous passage from England, our ship was cast away the 15th of December last, a hundred and fifty miles from the coast of Philadelphia. By Providence we were all but six saved by a sloop accidentally coming to take us up. My fate like that of the rest, was to save nothing but my bare life, and as I'm here among a poor people that can afford little or no relief, so I'm destitute of all manner of necessaries for my office and function."[30] The writer is not an Anglican parson but a Swedish Lutheran missionary named Gabriel Falk. There was, however, felt to be such an intimate connection between the Swedish and Anglican churches that the Soci-

27. Pascoe, p. 12.
28. *Ibid*, p. 841.
29. An Abstract of Mr. Cordiner's Journal, p. 1.
30. Fulham Papers, 9/60. Gabriel Falk, Philadelphia, March 8th, 1733.

ety had no hesitation in ordering "that twenty pounds should be given to Mr. Falk and the same is paid to Mr. Serenins, of which Mr. Falk has been acquainted by Dr. Humphreys."[31] Archibald Cumming now takes up the tale. Herr Falk has introduced himself to him, but perhaps the Swede does not speak English as well as he writes it, and Cumming is left with the idea that his name is Afflick. The different dates the two gentlemen use in their letters are worth noting. Cumming, an American, is still in the year 1732, while Falk, who of course uses the continental system of dating, has gone on to 1733. "Mr. Afflick," says Cumming, "the Swedish missionary who brought me your letter, offers his duty to your Lordship. The ship in which he came was cast away, and, poor gentleman, he lost all his clothes, books, etc. He made me promise to mention his necessities to the Society and to crave some small assistance.

"There was a Welsh clergyman, one Hugh Hughes, passenger in the same ship, but he died through the extremity of cold just as he came on shore at the mouth of our river. Your Lordship's licence of the province of New York was found in his pockets."[32] It is to be hoped that they recognized the signature, where Mr. Hughes had gone.

Altogether it is difficult to overestimate the dangers of the voyage. The missionary who had nothing worse to report than: "we had a very tedious and troublesome passage over, and were near thirteen weeks at sea,"[33] was fortunate. He who could write, "After a prosperous voyage, though interrupted with many delays, we arrived safe in Maryland the beginning of August last,"[34] was to be congratulated. Only very occasionally did anyone commit to paper the

31. *Ibid.*
32. Fulham Papers, 9/146.
33. *Ibid.*, 9/75. Philadelphia, October 19th, 1726.
34. *Ibid.*, 9?/192.

sentiment that he had enjoyed the voyage, although one commissary said: "I arrived here about the middle of April last after a fine, pleasant passage."[35] A clergyman in America calculated the cost of a voyage across the Atlantic as being about twenty-five pounds sterling, and remarked, "Such a sum, great as it is, is but a trifle in comparison to loss of time, risks at sea, and other discouragements, which frighten many well disposed persons."[36] Pascoe puts the cost of the voyage far higher, at a hundred pounds in fact.

A final hazard awaited the missionaries before they landed in America, the chance of being captured by pirates. Perhaps missionaries were more likely to be stopped on a return voyage to England, but there was nothing to hinder their falling in with some of the brethren of the coast on their voyage out. The early American pirates are attractive in many ways. Enjoying the virility of a government that arises from democratically elected rulers (the first in these parts), they were not the mere cutthroats that heavily property-conscious writers have represented but a section of the American colonies in misdirected revolt against the agency that had originally pried them from their mainland occupation as buccaneers—a revolt symbolized by their adoption of the red flag as their national emblem.[37] At their worst they were merely fighting for a living; at their best their restrained conduct (to their women prisoners for example) contrasts favorably with that displayed by the regular European navies. One thinks of the British at the capture of Gibraltar in this connection.[38] Discerning students must admit that many of the exploits in which the

---

35. *Ibid.*, 25/82, Patuxent in Maryland, August 12th, 1730.
36. *Ibid.*, 9/32. Philadelphia, November 14th, 1766.
37. Also displayed by those other early Americans, the Red Indians, with the same intention—to indicate "No Surrender."
38. Where terrible ill-treatment of the civilian population took place during the capture, according to Spanish accounts.

pirates engaged displayed as much bravery as those undertaken by the national fleets of the countries that made up
the pirate population for less worthy, if more high-
sounding ends.

Though pirates were likely to do the traveling clergy little
harm personally, being most of them good Protestants, and
some of them being desirous to have chaplains aboard their
ships, the missionaries might find their baggage overhauled
after an encounter with them. "Had we not been rifled by
the pirates," writes an unknown correspondent, who because of his severe tone toward the clergy must be assumed
to be a clergyman himself, "I had brought you a letter
signed by several gentlemen in Maryland, who suspecting
Mr. Henderson, thought it necessary to give the gentleman's character to let you know how unfit he is to bear any
office in church or state."[39] One is almost tempted to believe
that the pirate in question read the letter and pitched it and
the rest of the informer's baggage overboard in disgust.
Certainly it is difficult to see what he would want with a
parson's papers, or indeed his other effects. Bartholomew
Roberts, an American pirate of the time, released a clerical
prisoner without taking anything from him except four of
the articles of his office—three prayer books and a
corkscrew. The pirate, while disliking informers, may have
known Henderson personally and liked him, for part of the
business of piracy consisted in occasionally carrying letters
to the Bishop of London. "I now transmit to your grace
duplicates of what I sent by a pirate ship the fourteenth of
July last, viz. the letter of Assembly to your Grace."[40] It is
tempting to find in the Bishop's messenger on this occasion
the famous Captain John Avery who, about the time of this

39. No number, October 26th, 1725, endorsed "an unknown hand."
40. 9?/143. Francis Nicholson. Maryland, Port of Annapolis, February 13th,
1696.

letter made his last voyage to Britain to die brokenhearted at the dishonesty of the Bristol merchants to whom he had entrusted his hoard of diamonds, only to get nothing in return, but Avery appears to have sailed from Boston without touching at Maryland. It seems necessary to come to the conclusion that here we have a Maryland pirate who has escaped the historians. Even the contemporary census-taker of pirates, Edward Randolph, Surveyor General of Customs in the American colonies, who in the following year, 1696, drew up a report entitled "A discourse about pirates with proper remedies to suppress them,"[41] giving a list of the American pirate harbors, does not know anything about pirates in Maryland.

It is perhaps worth noticing, in conclusion, that the contacts between pirates and parsons did not begin and end at sea. No doubt many pirates, holidaying or careening upon the American mainland as Avery and Blackbeard did, may have gone to hear the missionaries preach and, edified by a glimpse of the Greater Purpose, returned refreshed to the drudgery of everyday life.

41. Philip Gosse, *The History of Piracy* (London: Green & Co., 1932), p. 320.

2

Each Returning Day

*M*OST of the missionaries seem to have been genuinely
delighted to see their new home. It would in any case
have been difficult not to rejoice at treading land after a
three months' voyage in a sailing ship, but this natural
feeling of elation was allied with a delight in the spontane-
ous enthusiasm of the Americans at the sight of ministers of
their own religion, a thing that some of them had not seen
for very many years. "At my first arrival in the country,"
said a missionary, "I had such kind invitations from the
several inhabitants that gave me reason to believe that nothing but the good I expected would result from such a well
disposed people as I experimentally found 'em to be.
Wherever I preached I had great numbers of hearers, but
in time of divine service observed most of 'em strangers to
the method of worship of our church. They brought many
of their children to be baptised, and what most surpised me,

found all of 'em pretty far advanced in years at their receiving the benefit of that sacrament."[1] It is worth noting that our first reaction to the Americans written home from the country comes from what might be described as a frontier parish *par excellence*, Chowan, in North Carolina. Although attractive to its new incumbent, as we have seen, it was one of the hardest parts of North America for a missionary to settle in. Two parsons, the first the Society had sent out to the Province, Adams and Gordon, had decided to return to Britain, discouraged by the wildness of the settlement, the poverty of the people, who were unable give him enough to live on, and the opposition of the Quakers.[2] More discouraging still was the fear of massacre by the Indians. More will be said about the relations of the missionaries with the Indians later, but it is impossible not to be continually referring to them, since they formed part of the backdrop against which life in the colonies was played out. North Carolina was suffering all the horrors of an Indian war when the writer of the letter, Ransford, took up his ministry. A hundred and thirty-seven settlers had just been massacred at Roanoak, and in spite of their defeat at the hands of Barnwell and the South Carolina forces, the Tuscaroras and their allies remained strong enough to kill eighty of the settlers in five years. In 1713 they captured Ransford himself, but he was able to escape and return to his parish of Chowan after seeking refuge in Virginia for two months. There he tried to effect the conversion of the friendly Chowan Indians before resigning in 1714.[3] The North Carolinians were genuinely anxious to have ministers among them, even though they could contribute little to their support. Arriving some fifty years later, Theodorus

1. 10/38. (G. Ransford), Chowan in North Carolina, July 25th 1712.
2. Pascoe, pp. 21, 22.
3. Pascoe, p. 22.

Swaine Drage found a similar warm welcome. "I arrived in this province," he wrote, "after a long passage attended with much hard weather and contrary winds, having been ten days on an island called Conebank Island. The people are at a great distance from a church. On their application, I gave private baptism to fifteen children. They offered me a gratuity for baptism, which I did not accept, but gave them certificates."[4] The governor showed him every civility, and offered him the choice of any parish he liked, warning him as he did so that "from an artful penning of the law," he could not induct him before the vestry approved of him as their minister. Drage adds that he has softened down the Governor's expressions of esteem in relaying them in this letter, for "there are many dissenters and it might encourage an opposition.

"It is an excessive fine climate, and beautiful country, and therefore many settlers [come] there from Pensilvania and the Jerseys."

A hearty welcome seems to have been the experience of the great majority of missionaries. "I have met with more civilities than I had reason to expect among so divided[5] a people," wrote Archibald Cumming to the Bishop.[6] Mr. Palmer, the missionary at Newhaven, remarked that "since he came here the people have been kind, and done everything they could for his comfort, the prosperity of the church and the advancement of religion. They have purchased a piece of ground in a convenient place and at the expense of about a hundred pound lawful money [i.e., not

4. 10/39. Theodorus Swaine Drage, Newburn, North Carolina, November 23rd., 1769. He afterwards took St. Luke's parish, Rowan County. *Ibid*., p. 850.
5. That is, in a population containing so many non-Anglicans.
6. 9/66 A. Cummings, Philadelphia, December 15th, 1726 (but see his letter of two months earlier).

colonial money] completely finished a house which they design for the church for ever."[7]

Unlike England, America did not have nearly so many clergymen as she needed. Even at the end of the colonial period there were only seventy-seven Society missionaries in the whole country,[8] and it was never possible, as in London, to walk into a coffee house and see two dozen or so at the same time. They were, accordingly, valued as a rarity. "I do assure your Lordship," remarked one incumbent, "that I never knew any place in all my life where a minister has had more honour and respect paid to him than the people are generally found to express here ."[9] Here and there, however, sour notes entered the paean of praise. "I have been here so short a time," said a clergyman, "that all the account I can give of this place is that the soil and clime seem to be better and more regular than the temper of the people."[10]

"His Excellency the Governor," said a Maryland parson, "was for sending me over the bay to the Eastern Shore, where I should be devoured by musquitoes, a dreadful kind of insects, by day, and by chinches, like our bugs in England, by night."[11] There was no facade of respectability, as in England, to conceal the poverty of the newer colonies. When a community was undergoing hard times, usually everyone had to share them, and the parsons often reacted violently to ways of life different from those to which they

7. This appears to have been Mr. Solomon Palmer, M.A. of Yale College, Connecticut, the former teacher at Yale College whose conversion to Anglicanism was one of the chief S.P.G. trophies. He was, then, an American and not newly arrived in the country. Newhaven, Connecticut, Dec. 1, 1763.
8. Pascoe, p. 79.
9. 9?/66.
10. A. Cumming, Philadelphia, Pennsylvania, October 19th, 1726. 9/75.
11. 21/119.

were accustomed. A parson in South Carolina wrote to complain that "the victuals of the country are not less hard than the climate. The bread is made of Indian corn boiled in water. We have but once a week fresh beef, but the heat is so great that it can be made use of but one day. We have no other liquor but rum. We mix it with water, a pernicious liquor that kills many that drinks to excess."[12] Other causes of complaint were the climate and the fever in the south. Some missionaries seem to have received a totally unreal picture of what life in the colonies would be like, and were unable to face the hardships of the life that they had undertaken, as the number of resignations after a year or two's service show. Some felt that they could not stand the climate another year, and begged to be allowed to go home; on the other hand, it is only fair to mention that one or two of the West Indian missionaries came north to America because they could not endure the "torrid clime" in Barbados or some other island.

If the newcomer were a commissary, or otherwise accredited representative of the Bishop, he would not have to look around very far for trouble. In Maryland, for instance, the Local Assembly had attempted to cut down salaries of ministers in 1729, and the Society had exerted its influence to try to counteract this act. This caused trouble when an emissary of the Bishop's arrived in the colony in 1730. "A fine passage," he remarked, in describing his experiences, "but the reception I had was not so pleasant. Some of our leading libertines had spirited up the people against me, inasmuch [sic] that they threatened to mob me. Indeed one ruffian meeting me at a gentleman's house struck me twice, after which I must confess I struck him. Another, no less

12. 10/12. J. Adam de Martel, Lurisburg, In South Carolina, July 13th, 1769 (not mentioned in Pascoe).

than a Justice of the Peace and an Assembly Man, beat two clergymen, Mr. Robertson and Mr. Fletcher. The clergy in a body complained of the latter to the Governor, but it does not appear that he takes any notice of it. Nay he was so far from resenting that barbarous usage that in two or three days after he threatened in public company that he would kick me, though he has always spoke fair to my face. Such hard usage have the clergy here for defending the patrimony of the Church against the incroachments of the people."[13] It was perhaps a little idealistic in the Local Assembly to expect that the clergy should labor on a reduced salary. Nevertheless, the attitude of the assembly represents a carryover from what was felt on the same subject. Tithing was looked on as one of the most unjust of the feudal burdens and people continued to object to it to our own day. An old harvest home song, still sung, sums up the viewpoint of the tithe payer:

> We've cheated the parson, we'll cheat him again,
> For why should the rascal have one in ten?

While it was comparatively easy in England to bring a parishioner who refused to pay to reason by excommunicating him, waiting forty days and then having him arrested by the sheriff or justice of peace on a *significavit*, which meant that he would stay in jail till he paid, it was much more difficult, not to say impossible, to deal with noncontributors in America. Hence the disturbances in Maryland, in which I will round off with the stories of Mr. Fletcher and Mr. Roberts, who have been already referred to, although they were, in fact, not newly arrived ministers. "On March the fifth 1729," recalls Thomas Fletcher, "Mr. Sloughtone meeting with me in Stepney parish in Somerset County, I

13. Maryland Box /3 Patuxent in Maryland, August 12th, 1730.

taxed him of an advantage he had taken of me at the house of a certain Thomas Holebrook in the aforesaid county, saying there, that if a man had murdered his father and committed incest with his mother and sister, if a man was poor, I would take his part. At several times also he passed scandalous reflections on the whole body of the clergy of Maryland, saying that they were a scandal to the aforesaid province, and on March the fifth as aforesaid challenged me [i.e.,to a duel] and afterwards further abused me by striking of me."[14] Now James Robertson takes up the sad tale. "Sometime last March Colonel Elzey of Somerset County being dangerously sick, sent for me. Upon my coming to him he was desirous to receive the sacrament, in order to which I proposed the necessity of a reconciliation between him and Mr. William Sloughton, his son in law, which he told me he was willing to, and desired Mr. Sloughton might come to see him. Some few days after, viz. the eleventh of April, I went to see Colonel Elzey where Mr. Sloughton happened to be, and after some conversation with Colonel Elzey and praying for him in the presence of the said Mr. William Sloughtone, who seemed very much affected and serious all the while, the said Mr. Sloughtone immediately asked me to walk out with him a little, pretending (as I imagined) friendship or some private business, and before had well wiped the tears (out) of his eyes, he fell a beating and abusing me till (before I was aware of his design) he *blinded me of one eye* and bruised my face to that degree that the marks of his blows remained black and blue for three weeks. And presently after his using me so barbarously he was so far from expressing any sorrow for it that he said 'if I was the Archbisop of Canterbury he would serve me the same sauce, and that he would beat all the

---

14. Maryland Box. James Robertson, May 22nd, 1730.

clergy in the country, one after another, if they durst presume to talk any thing of him.'"[15] The Bishop's pen squeaked as he underlined the italicized passage and no doubt he squeaked himself when he read the sentence about the Archbishop of Canterbury. It seems from the writing, which appears to be normal, that the injury to Robertson's eye may have been temporary. All these troubles, for newcomers as well as for long stayers, were aggravated by the absence of a bishop. A prelate in America would have stood up to squires like Sloughtone, who objected to clergymen's championing poor men, or to being checked for immoral conduct, and have seen that the sheriff brought him to account for his brutal habits.

Sometimes the wherewithal to support a minister was so small and the material welcome so cold that the desire to turn about and go home (often the most sensible thing that could be done) was irresistible. Urmston's claim that he and his family in North Carolina "have lived many a day only on a dry crust and a draught of salt water out of the Sound"[16] can hardly be accepted at its face value, but there is no reason to doubt that he and his family were often in considerable want. It is however, difficult to see a frontier community like the one in which Urmston lived actually letting him starve. Here as elsewhere there may have been intentional exaggeration in order to secure a bounty from the Society. When therefore Urmston writes, a few years after his arrival in the country, in 1712, to say "If the Society is not kind I shall be forced to run for it, bankrupt, and not able to continue much longer here," it is necessary to take his remarks with a grain of salt. When he makes a statement in the same letter that can be proved to be untrue, "Mr.

15. 3/30. James Robertson, May 22nd, 1730. Neither of these clergymen appears to be known to Pascoe.
16. Pascoe, p. 22.

Ransford hath preached but once in this government and I
hear is bound for England per ye first ship. He hath earned
an hundred and fifty pound easily,"[17] it is easy to see how
Urmston fell into disrepute even with the rather easily
gulled Society, and had to go to be a parson in Maryland
where bad clergymen were the norm.

The settling-in pains of a missionary were likely to be
extended if he arrived in a part of the country suffering
from a minor civil war, which was the fate of South Carolina
during part of this period. The conditions of the state drew
from a correspondent a full report to the Bishop. Part of the
trouble, as another letter writer remarked, was that South
Carolina had too many lawyers and not enough law.

"For many years past," said the writer, "the back parts of
this Province hath been infested with an infernal gang of
villains, who have committed such horrid depredations on
our properties and estates, such insults on the persons of
many settlers, and perpetrated such shocking outrages
throughout the back settlements as is past description." He
then began to describe them. "Our large stocks of cattle are
either stolen or destroyed, our Cow Pens are broke up, and
all our valuable horses are carried off. Houses have been
burned by these rogues and families stripped and turned
naked into the woods. Stores have been broken open and
rifled by them wherefrom several traders are absolutely
ruined. Private houses have been plundered and the inhabitants wantonly tortured in the Indian manner for to be
made [to] confess where they secreted their effect from
plunder. Married women have been ravished, virgins de-
flowered, and other unheard of cruelties committed by
these barbarous ruffians who by being let loose amongst us
(and connived at) by the acting magistrates (and) have
hereby reduced numbers of individuals to poverty.

17. Pascoe, p. 22, 10/40, John Urmston, 1712.

"No trading persons, or with money or goods dare keep cash or any valuable articles by them, nor can women stir abroad, but with a guard or in terror. The chastity of many beauteous maidens have [*sic*] been threatened by these rogues. Merchants' stores are obliged for to be kept constantly guarded (which enhances the price of goods) and thus we live, not as under a British Government, every man sitting in peace and security under his own vine, and his own fig tree, but as if [we] were in *Hungary* or *Germany* and in a state of war, continually exposed to the incursions of *Hussars* and *Pandours*." There was no hope, he added, of getting any of these banditti punished by the normal process of law. If captured, they were simply pardoned through the connivance of the magistrates. "Thus distressed, thus situated, unrelieved by Government, many among us have been obliged to punish some of these banditti, and their accomplices in a proper manner, NECESSITY (that first principle) compelling them to do what was expected that the executive branch of the legislature would *long ago* have done.

"We are *Free men*—British subjects, not born *slaves*—we contribute our proportion in all public taxations and discharge our duty to the public, equally with our fellow provincials, yet we do not participate with them in the rights and benefits which they enjoy, though equally entitled to them. [We are] obliged to defend our families by our own strength. As *legal methods* are beyond our reach or not as yet extended to us."[18] The fact that the tobacco barns were likely to go up in flames at any moment, incidentally, meant that it would be difficult for a parson in South Carolina to collect any stipend, since this was paid in leaf tobacco. Another hand now takes up the task of describing South

18. 9?/72. (Copy of) "The Remonstrance presented to the Comon's House of Assembly by the upper inhabitants, 1767," p. 2.

Carolina's bleeding wounds to the Bishop. Like the former writer, he takes the view that the "Regulators," the citizens who were acting illegally against the bandits in the absence of any movement from the atrophied legal system of the state, were not dangerous sectional interests, but merely fearless vigilantes eager for their country's peace.

"As ye people could not have protection from ye laws," he says, "nor those in authority, necessity obliged them (first) to associate in families for mutual defence. But that method proving ineffectual (as ye rogues would go in gangs of fifteen or twenty well armed) the whole country at length rose in a body and drove off the villains, burning of their cabins and camps, taking away the goods and horses and young girls they had carried off. Many battles were fought and persons killed on both sides—while ye Government did nothing—silently looked on, publishing proclamations— some against the rogues—others against the mob. The rogues at length began to fire houses likewise. This got the mob to consider of some order in their proceedings, who chose a thousand men to execute the laws against all villains and the harbourers of villains. These men assumed the title of 'Regulators,' they pulled down the houses of all who had entertained, secreted, abetted and supported these gangs of thieves, whipped the magistrates who went snacks [19] with them, in their plunder and protected them, broke up ye brothels where they had their nocturnal revels, and where they used to carry and deflower the prettiest girls they could seduce or lay hold on. All worthy of death they sent down to the Provost Marshal, all who promised amendment and were petty rogues they whipped. The women they ducked and exposed. And at length secured and gave peace to the community, doing more in three months than the executive

19. I.e., went halves.

power had effected in twenty years and what (but for them) would never have been done."[20]

When it is remembered that the Indians of South Carolina, the Appalachis, Callabaws, Creeks, and Yammonsees, had begun a war of extermination with the white settlers in 1715, and that from 1747 to 1767 the Regulator trouble was going on, it will be seen that the newly arrived minister in the state had little on which to congratulate himself, and this applied equally to other ministers who began their incumbency during an Indian war.

The material conditions, and consequently the life, of the missionaries varied much. Some of them, as we have seen, were very poor. Others were very rich. Richard Ludlam of Goose Creek, South Carolina, for instance, was able to leave two thousand pounds to the S.P.G., and he was by no means an isolated example of a missionary with money.[21] Whether those who had money brought it with them from Britain, or earned it through quietly saving their stipends is difficult to say, but there is certainly a great air of comfort in the lives of some of the parsons of the time. Much depended, for a clergyman's prospects, on whether he could lay hands on some coined money. Many ministers in the South complained that they never saw any, because their stipends were paid entirely in tobacco, the chief medium of exchange in certain states. There were, however, some things that it would not buy, such as British-made clothes. A parson's comfort was likely to be increased if he could turn his stipend into some kind of money. British "legal" currency was usually too much to hope for, but there was always the possibility of selling some of the leaf for the colonial *assignats*, bank bills that were, however, not so much money as

20. South Carolina Box.
21. Pascoe, p. 850.

wallpaper. Because the tobacco stipend in which ministers were paid in the growing states of the South was reckoned according to a poll tax that levied so much tobacco on every "taxable" person in the county or parish, livings were reckoned according to the amount of leaf with which they were accredited. Great animosity was aroused over the question of who was a "taxable"; were Quakers and Negro slaves to be accounted so? The Anglican parsons, with an intransigence as remarkable as it was unconscious, claimed that Quakers ought to contribute to *their* support in the South, just as in the North, where the Nonconformists were strong, they regarded it as the greatest injustice that Anglican church members should be compelled to pay taxes toward the support of the Congregationalist or Presbyterian minister of their district. The price of tobacco varied from year to year, according to what it was fetching in England, which a tyrannical King and Parliament had compelled to smoke nothing but American tobacco, but as we have seen, it was generally falling downwards during the eighteenth century. Owing to the fluctuation, many parsons could not, or pretended they could not, ascertain the value of their livings. "I can't ascertain the value of my living," remarked one Maryland minister, as he filled in a questionnaire for the Bishop, which will be referred to again, "it being paid in tobacco, which is an uncertain commodity, and the number of taxables sometimes more, sometimes less."[22] Another was more specific and more bitter. "The value of my living is not in sterling money. It arises in tobacco. This present year it is forty seven thousand, three hundred and sixty pounds of tobacco (never so much before) and when the sheriffs' and clerks' salaries are de-

---

22. 25/5. Answer to printed questionnaire from B. of L. sent to John Donaldson, King and Queen parish, St. Marys and Charles County, Maryland (not known to Pascoe).

ducted out of it, besides what the law has taken from me against my consent, and my parishioners (if your Lordship allows it) the remainder, turned into sterling money will be near sixty pounds, as tobacco goes now."[23] The incumbent of Coventry parish in Somerset county, Maryland, declared that "our living arises from forty pounds of tobacco levied on each taxable. The number of the taxables and also the price of the tobacco is very variable. This present year it is in this country four shillings sterling in British goods at first cost, at which price my living amounts to forty six pounds sterling. But at this country we seldom can have money or bills for it."[24] Some idea of the fluctuation of the value of livings can be got from the following statement of a Maryland incumbent. "My benefice is in tobacco, which makes it impossible to rate it certain in sterling money. Sometimes I make two hundred pounds a year sterling of it, and sometimes not sixty, but oftener between the two sums, as tobacco rates in England."[25] Tobacco was an expensive commodity in England, and it is not difficult to imagine a young prospective minister receiving a letter from an American parish asking him to come there and officate, and mentioning that it was worth "20,000 pounds of tobacco a year to a minister besides his perquisites, marriages, funeral sermons, etc."[26] If the candidate valued this amount of tobacco according to what it would fetch in England, he might have been pardoned for thinking he was to come into not only an assured, but a handsome income. As we shall see, however, tobacco became a really valuable commodity only after the customs and the English merchants had got their hands on

23. 25/2. William Tibbs, rector. May 29th, 1724. Pascoe, p. 851, mentions him as the missionary at St. Paul's Baltimore, in 1705.
24. 25/17. James Robertson, Coventry parish in Somerset County (unknown to Pascoe).
25. 25/84. Jacob Henderson.
26. 3/206. Somerset County in Maryland, June 31st, 1721.

it. If the S.P.G. did not nourish these misconceptions on the part of candidates, they seem to have done little to dispel them. Some members of the hierarchy, when consulted by a young hopeful, might drop a shrewd hint to the effect that perhaps prospects in the colonies were not quite so rosy as they appeared, but on the whole many missionaries went overseas with a totally false conception of what their future would be like. It is not surprising that the zeal of many of them to go to America was equaled only by their zeal to leave it, shortly afterwards. Of course the Society could always cloud the issue by pointing to various missionaries and saying "They are comfortable, if not rich, far richer than they could have been in England."

The amount of tobacco paid to ministers varied with the different states. George Murdoch remarks that "the clergy are much better provided for there, [in Maryland] than here" [in Virginia]. They have 40 pound of tobacco per poll. Here we have sixteen thousand pounds tobacco per annum, which doth not amount to so much by a great deal. They are all inducted there; here very few. The place where I am is a very poor place and remote from trade, and though we have all alike in every parish, yet tobacco is of very little value in such places as are remote from navigable rivers."[27] He might have added that in Virginia there was a sharp distinction between those who were paid in "scented tobacco" and those who had to accept the less-sought-after Aranoka grade. Even in Maryland the parsons were fortunate indeed if they were paid their stipend in tobacco that could be sold in London as "right Virginny." "Tobacco," noted a parson, "being ye one and only staple commodity of ye country is that out of which our small incomes are paid. The manner of which is this. Every planter for himself and

27. 3/95. Maryland,

his male children and white servant men; as also for his negro slaves (both male and female) after their age of sixteen years, forty pound of tobacco per poll, demandable in the winter quarter, upon execution by the Sheriff, five pound in the hundred being deducted for his trouble in collecting it, and a thousand pounds, by a late Act of Assembly, being also deducted towards ye maintenance of a parish and vestry clerk. But some of us are forced to give two thousand pounds to the clerks, by reason of their going so far to do their duties on ye Lord's Day.

"The tobacco which is raised by the public levy of forty pound per poll, [for] some secular offices and other charges of the country is generally slighted by the English merchants, being reckoned (when received) to be worth about one fourth part of that (quantity to quantity) which the planters cure (as they term it) or manage for their own freight and sale. The reason for which ye public tobacco is generally slighted is that ye planters cull ye best of their crop for their own freighting or selling it for goods or bills of exchange, and keep ye refuse and discoloured tobacco to pay ye sheriffs for their taxes and duties.

"The merchants are not for meddling with this tobacco; not only because it is much worse than ye other, but because it is generally very troublesome to them to get it paid in any reasonable time, and that often they cannot get it at all, wholly losing their time and labour in going from place to place to demand it of those planters to whom the Sheriffs send them. This is a great and inevitable damage and sometimes a total disappointment of such as had their dependence on the public pay of ye country."[28]

Not surprisingly, when we come to see the difficulties that awaited a parson who wanted to send his own often-inferior

28. 3/145. May 14th, 17. *Ibid*., Annapolis, Maryland.

stipend tobacco to the European market, many of the missionaries felt that their official salary was almost worthless. Sometimes it could not be raised at all; if it could be, it was of little value; with it they could buy few of the things that were essential to a frontier settler: powder and shot for hunting, woolen homemade clothes that would keep out of the cold of a continental winter, the clerical uniform without which no parson was decent, medicine, and all the other things that were made in the colonies and could only be purchased, in them, for some form of hard currency. It became the ambition of every southern parson to own a plantation of his own, which he could work himself and raise good tobacco that would fetch a reasonable price from the tobacco brokers. In order to run a plantation he had to have slaves, and to get slaves he needed capital. "I design a plantation of my own," wrote the Bishop's Commissary, "for my successors."[29] The original three Anglican parsons in Maryland, "having made a hard shift to live here for some time after they came hither, did afterwards marry and maintain their families out of the plantations they had with their wives."[30] In fact, the parsons got hold of their capital by marrying American girls with dowries consisting of large tracts of land with their attached slaves. At a stroke of the wedding bell they had become independent of their vestries.

This meant that the southern parsons had at once become much more identified with their wealthier parishioners. They had become planters themselves, with a stake in the country. Whether the fact that they now had a large number of their fellow mortals locked up in the barracoons was going to influence their views on the slavery question is

29. Jacob Henderson, 25/184.
30. 3/145. May 14th 17. Annapolis, Maryland.

difficult to say, but what can be postulated is that it was this alliance with the land owning class that ensured that the Anglican church in the South was going to rebel against Britain in the Revolution. Whereas the Northern Anglican clerics exhibited many edifying instances of loyalty to the British and loyalist cause, it is fair to describe the Established Church, as Sweet does, as "divided" in the middle colonies, and "strongly American in the southern colonies, especially Virginia and Maryland."[31] Nor was this all; as the same writer points out, two thirds of the signers of the Declaration Of Independence were Anglicans, and six of them were sons or grandsons of Anglican clergymen. George Washington, James Madison, John Marshall, Patrick Henry, and Alexander Hamilton were all members of a church that deplored the use of force even against a tyrannical government, preached the doctrine of nonresistance, regarded the King as the Head of the Church, and taught that rebellion was as the sin of witchcraft. The S.P.G. missionaries were untainted with revolutionary doctrine for the most part, at least in the North. The rector of Trinity Church, New York, reported that those in New Jersey, New York, and Connecticut were all "faithful, loyal subjects."[32] Anglican parsons were expected to be red-hot monarchists. "I have in all respects found him," writes Governor Francis Nicholson about parson Lawrence, "a very pious and zealous son of the Church of England, a constant assertor of monarchy (which I think is a natural consequence of the former), and wholly devoted to his Majesty's interest."[33] "It is undoubtedly the wish," writes William Smith, "indeed too openly avowed, of some in this country to have the Church

---

31. W. W. Sweet, *The Story of Religions in America*, p. 256.
32. *Ibid*., p. 254.
33. 3/190.

clergy considered as tools of power, slavish in their tenets, and privately enemies to the principles of the Revolution" (i.e., the "glorious revolution" of 1688, in England).[34] Henry Harris found occasion to remark to William Dummer, Lieutenant Governor of Massachusetts, that in a sermon in King's Chapel, he "exposed the pernicious tendency of certain tenets and principles which are now under the censure of the government, and directly strike at our most gracious sovereign's parliamentary right to the crown of Great Britain. I find," he went on, "that the faithful discharge of my duty to God and the King has drawn upon me the displeasure of some persons who have expressed themselves with much indecent warmth respecting me."[35]

The fact that there should be found Anglicans and Anglican parsons who were prepared to espouse just the opposite of the principles expressed above is to be attributed, not only to their identification with the planter class, but to the fact that many Southern parsons had married American wives. In doing so, they had to a greater or less degree acquired patriotic principles from their bedfellows. Nobody is likely to preach from his pulpit what he would not maintain at his breakfast table, and the country wives Americanized the missionaries to such an extent that they undermined the loyalty, to the crown, of the whole of the South.

The Assembly's petition, which I have already quoted, went on to say that:"The merchants will allow us at prime cost very rarely a penny and sometimes but an half penny or farthing a pound for our tobacco in bartering with them [which] will hardly (supply) us with clothes and other necessaries. If we have any over plus, when our necessities and

34. 9/112. William Smith? Philadelphia, July 8th, 1775.
35. 6/23. April 24th, 1724. H. Harris to William Dummer, Esq., Lieutenant Governor of Massachusetts.

conveniencies are served, its hazardous for us to freight it,
lest it should prove a drug in the English or Holland market, and by paying from ten, sometimes to sixteen pound
sterling per tun for freight, besides the King's custom,
etc."[36] A combined marketing association to sell the parsons' tobacco, which might have solved all their difficulties,
was impossible owing to the distance between the parishes,
and the lack of the necessary capital to start it. In spite of
their frequent complaints about the conduct of business by
the tobacco merchants, their dealings with them led in one
instance at least to a London tobacco merchant's becoming
an agent for a missionary. Thus Hugh James told the
Bishop: "If your Lordship shall vouchsafe to write to me,
please to lodge your letter with Mr. Lawrence Williams,
tobacco merchant in London."[37] This is just the sort of
business friendship one would expect to exist (especially
between two Welshmen). Similarly, in French Canada, as
has been described elsewhere,[38] the *habitants* formed
friendships with the Paris fur merchants, who bought much
of their produce, and these furriers sometimes had Canadian children to stay with them while they did their schooling in France.

Deeply indignant as the clergy were at being unable to
realize a fair price from their tobacco stipend, those in
Maryland grew even more indignant at the passing of an
Act of Assembly on 21st May, 1730, called "An Act for
improveing the staple of tobacco, etc." By this act
parishioners were legally enabled to pay the clergy a quarter of their salaries in grain, at the rate of forty-two pounds
of tobacco per bushel of wheat. Clerical comment on this
measure was as follows: "The equivalent pretended to be

36. 3/145.
37. 25/47.
38. "Some Acadian Letters," *Journal of the Society of Archivists* 1, no. 4 (1959).

given by the act bears no proportion to the commodity deducted. The people may pay which of the sorts of grain they please. Oats will (in all probability) be their choice, because they are of least value and easily raised. There is no use made of them, but to feed horses, so that they must lie by and rot except by chance they can barter them away for rum, which they must sell out again for money or tobacco, and how unbecoming a clergyman will it appear to see a rum store at every parsonage for the encouragement of sots and drunkards. Physicians, tradesmen, and servants are under no obligation to take part of their debts or wages in these commodities. To support these and other expenses was hard enough on the clergy before, but now it will be intolerable."[39] "Our establishment," said a parson, "which we judged very secure, by having the royal assent, is now by Act of Assembly broken in upon, and our maintenance reduced under a pretence of enlarging it, for under colour of advancing the price of tobacco by restricting our parishioners from making too great quantities of it, they think it reasonable to take away one fourth part of our income, the forty pound of tobacco secured to every clergyman by the act of religion or to pay him at the rate of ten shillings current money, for it, which we look upon to be detrimental to us, as either taking away one fourth part of our income or else putting a determinate price on it, which will set us on a precarious foot, for should tobacco rise in price our parishioners will pay us in money and should tobacco prove good for little [we] will be sure to have it."[40]

For those ministers who had no plantation, conditions seem occasionally to have been severe, according to their own reports. "No house, a small glebe, but yet forest," wrote

39. Maryland, 21/139.
40. 21/94. November 24th, 1728.

one incumbent.[41] "I was at the charge to build and keep the buildings in repair at my own charges," said another, "Which has [been] and is chargeable to me."[42] A third notes that "I have a very indifferent glebe and an old ruinous house, not fit for me to occupy nor for any man to lease it."[43] "There is land for a glebe," comments a fourth, "but it's so poor that I never could get any person to live upon it."[44] The only person who seemed even fairly satisfied with his glebe described it as "An extraordinary glebe of four hundred acres left to the parish. The house is very indifferent, it has been repaired over and over. The vestry (I hope) will build a new one."[45] Reports such as "I have a house and glebe, but to no benefit to me as yet,"[46] and "My dwelling house is kept in repair at my own charges,"[47] are fairly typical ones. "Our parish in the case of glebes," wrote Henry Nichols, "has been very unfortunate. About eleven years ago one Colonel Smithson, a very grave and pious gentleman, left his dwelling plantation and five or six other tracts of land, eight negro slaves and considerable plate, for the use of the communion table. But by the fraud of his executrix all had been like to be defeated. He had, when he died, money enough in his house to pay all his debts which she, getting into her possession, concealed and brought the estate so much in debt that the negroes and plate were all swallowed up."[48] All these latter instances have been taken from Maryland, where there had been no long Anglican settlement. In Connecticut, where there had been Angli-

41. 25/11. Shrewsbury parish in Kent County, Maryland, June 1st, 1724.
42. 25/10. St. Peters parish in Talbot County, Maryland.
43. 25/17. James Robertson (mentioned before). Coventry parish in Somerset County, Maryland.
44. 20/25.
45. *Ibid.*
46. 20/22.
47. 25/22.
48. 21/71. Henry Nicols, July 16th, 1724.

cans if not parsons for some time, where the people had been settled longer and were in consequence more prosperous, matters were often different and the missionary at Newhaven could congratulate himself on a completely finished house built at a cost of a hundred pounds sterling.[49]

Not all parsons were "poor persons," however; one or two of them were rich men. Robert Maule, who ministered in South Carolina, left seven hundred and fifty pounds to the S.P.G. when he died in 1717, while Jacob Henderson, who comes into these pages a good deal, bequeathed a thousand pounds for the same purpose in 1751. Like the contemporary Anglican church in England the American church exhibited considerable contrasts of wealth and poverty side by side, though it is possible to suspect that the American parsons were never quite so badly off as some of their British colleagues. The immigrant clergymen did their best to create on the other side of the Atlantic that atmosphere of refined comfort which the better-to-do of them enjoyed in Britain. Here, for example, is a description of the holding of Parson Giles Rainsford, who has been already mentioned under the alternative spelling of his name, Ransford, in this book. Rainsford is apparently settled in Maryland, after coming north from bad Indian country in Chowan. How much of his furniture and effects he had with him in North Carolina is difficult to say, but most of his effects could only have been procured from England. It is not, surely, a slight to the contemporary arts in Maryland to assume that Rainsford might have found it difficult to hang his walls with local paintings. Consequently it is necessary to think of Rainsford sitting in a sort of oasis of Augustan elegance in the track of a Tuscarora war party. Like most British

49. L.P.L., 124/2/232.

people, and unlike the French in Canada, for example, Rainsford saw no purpose in living like the Indians. He was going to have a still life on one wall even if he had to have a loophole in the other. Focusing on the contemporary drawings of houses in the tobacco colonies with one part of the mind, and on this inventory with another, it is possible to get a good idea of how Maryland parsons lived in those days. Rainsford had, at the time he sold out to Parson Eversfield: a hundred and seven acres of land with corn on it, a dwelling house of four rooms and a kitchen, a Corn House, a Smoke House, a Tobacco House, a Hen House, an old dwelling house, and House of Office, "as also one new cart, three troughs, a ladder, axe and spade." He owned sixteen thousand pound of tobacco at the rate of sixteen shillings per hundred (valued at forty-eight pounds) and "three countryborn negroes" (valued at eighty five pounds). The parson's stock consisted of "seven head of black cattle, nine sheep, six lambs, nine hogs, eight young pigs, together with a handsome parcel of corn and bacon [valued at twenty pounds], three horses, two mares and a colt [valued at twenty pounds], two side saddles and one man's saddle" [valued at twenty pounds]. He had besides "four tables, eight chairs, two dozen and two of pewter plates, five pewter dishes, two good feather beds with one new tick, two negroe beds, three pewter basins, one pewter porringer, four brass spoons, two pewter salt boles, six knives and forks, two iron pots, two brass skillets, one large brass kettle, one copper tea kettle, two tin kettles, four earthen pots, two handsome looking glasses, three brass candlesticks, two teapots, six coffee dishes with saucers, one bell metal mortar, one warming pan, one frying pan, one spit, a case with glass bottles in it, three drinking glasses, two dozen and a half of glass bottles, one glass salt cellar, one grid iron, six iron skewers, one large lantern, one pair of tongs and shovel, three canisters, one quart mug, one punch bowl, a chopping knife and axe, a box smoothing iron, a funnel, two hair brooms, one coat brush, two large bags, three bed studs[50] one tray, one pail, one colander, six petty pans, several handsome chests and boxes, one sixty gallon cask, three pipes containing a hundred gallons each, one beer barrel, ten pictures, two old negroe saddles, nine fleeces of wool, one searce[?], one sieve, two decanters, twenty gallons of mollasses, six small pictures, two old chairs, two crickets, three cocks, three hens, eight chickens."[51] The impression of tasteful comfort given by this inventory is increased by the possessions of other parsons, which included items such as "one cloth gown, and cassock, ten pounds, one canopy bedstead, curtains, etc., nine pounds."[52] While we may believe some of the parsons when they tell us that they are uncomfortable, they were probably never so pinched for the sheer necessities of life as their hungry colleagues in Ireland and parts of England. The lot of a parson in America was infinitely better than that of one in Presbyterian Scotland, for example, as George Macqueen, who became a Maryland parson, after having been "forced to fly from his native country by the Presbyterian persecution in Scotland,"[53] would have pointed out. No one was going to turn him out of house and home in the middle of a snowstorm in Maryland, as a Presbyterian magistrate might do in his homeland, and he would go on to tell you that given the choice between falling into the hands of an Indian war band and those of a party of Glenkindie's Dragoons, he would choose the former. The worst that could happen to a clergyman in the colonies was that he should have to work

50. Probably bedsteads.
51. 3/54.
52. 9/221. Philadelphia, September 11th, 1713.
53. Pascoe, p. 851.

the fields for a living in his own glebe or reclaimed holding. This was of course, the very last thing that some ministers wanted to do, but many Anglicans, sent out to the West Indies by Cromwell during the Civil War, had had to do it before them. Indeed, it is impossible to avoid contrasting the happier conditions enjoyed by the colonial parsons with those of their colleagues at home. If they occasionally got yellow fever or malaria, America, not crowded with people, was a far healthier place to live in than contemporary Great Britain, ravaged by smallpox and other epidemics. If they were really reduced to poverty, their neighbors would not let them starve to death. The trial of the last witch in England, Jane Wenham, arose partly because she was refused a turnip by a local farmer when she was so hungry as to be grubbing about in his field for something to eat. She cursed him and was brought to trial for casting a spell. Although acquitted and able to live out her old age as a pensioner in Hertingfordbury, it is pleasant to note that the spell subsequently took effect and the farmer in question was filled with buckshot by a public-spirited highwayman while driving to market some years later. It is difficult to imagine this incident taking place in America at this time (1712). The worship of that Unknown God of the eighteenth century, Property, had not taken deep enough root there, and the colonists, many of whom had known poverty for themselves, were more friendly toward poor people.

The many letters of the missionaries that indicate cases of extreme distress have to be taken with a certain amount of salt. Eighteenth-century clergy were expert at writing begging letters, as anyone who works through some of those sent to the Archbishop of York at this time will admit. There is no doubt that the parson who was actually out of a living might be hard put to it to support a wife and family on occasion. "My Lord," writes one such, "I had ye honour in my last to inform your Lordship about ye present state of Cape Fear both civil and ecclesiastical. I was the first minister of the church of England that came to these places to preach, which I did during three years and a half, and at last frustrated of ye best part of my salary I was obliged to ask for my discharge, then forced to work in the field to help to maintain my family afterward compelled by necessity to sell my house and land and lastly my moveables so that at this time I am no better than a mendicant. I have been three years out of place, depending and living upon my own substance, but every now and then exercising my functions gratis among some of ye dispersed families. 'Tis true, my Lord, I had several invitations from abroad for vacancies to be supplied but the letters directed to me fell into the hands of our gentlemen, who made no scruple to suppress them as I have found it out since, lest my complaints of their proceedings should reach too far. Last of all I went further northward to a new colony called New River, consisting of above one hundred families, all poor people but very desirous to have ye holy worship set up amongst them. Some of the chief inhabitants had already been secretly seduced by the favourers of one Chub, and by means of such seducers and underhand dealers many have learned to quibble and cavil about the holy scripture, and as their belief, so is their manner of life, in public incest or polygamy, the first of which in a great man was the first occasion of my gradual depression and degradation in their mind, when I spoke against it."[54] In another letter from North Carolina, from Richard Marsden, there is a protest about the high cost of living (in which the necessity for having sedan-chair carriers is stressed). Marsden was expelled from the Society in 1738

54. North Carolina Box /19. New Hanover, alias Cape Fear in North Carolina, April 23rd, 1734.

for "misconduct before he was established a Missionary under the Society's seal."[55] Possibly not so much his conduct as the fact that he was working as a merchant as well as a missionary, was objected to. In this letter, Marsden excuses his engaging in trade, and adds: "I have spent in the last two years above two hundred pounds [of] this currency, besides being often obliged to take two negroes for three or four days in a week to transport me where I am necessitated to preach, to ye great neglect of my plantation, which would be a certain maintenance if I could allow myself to continue at home. I am bold to say that there is not a clergyman in the West Indies or in this part of America that has a better title to the Society's favour than I have. I have never acted from worldly advantages and I go through more fatigue and labour in the discharge of my office than any three of them, and love is the spring and fountain of all my performances."[56] Marsden's character is drawn by a Huguenot missionary whose parishioners he had persuaded to have him for their minister instead of the Frenchman. He had been, according to John Lapierre, "a preacher in Charlestown in South Carolina, who declined to appear before Commissary Johnston to show his credentials, then Lord Portland's chaplain in Jamaica, an incumbent in Virginia after that, and of late a trafficant to Lisbon and sometime after his return promoted by a few gentlemen to be minister to Cape Fear without any popular election. A man of indifferent character and causing, by the violence of his assessments, great murmurings among the people."[57] A certain connection seems to exist between the fervency of the ap-

---

55. Pascoe, p. 859.
56. North Carolina Box, 7th July, 1735. Richard Marsden, from Cape Fear, North Carolina.
57. *Ibid.*/19. Lapierre is also known to have been relieved by the Society after the Indian War in 1715. Pascoe, p. 860.

peals for help on the part of a minister and his personal character. Quite often it is those who are subsequently disallowed by the Society, like Marsden, who put up the most convincing pleas that they need assistance. Here, for example, is a typical letter from John Urmston, who, after falling into disrepute with the S.P.G., was "burned to death in North Carolina," not, it is to be hoped, on the receipt of a writ *de heretico comburendo*.[58]

"This unhappy country! What difficulties and unheard of hardships I've here struggled with. I could not have fared worse in Malabar.[59] Our confusions have much obstructed my endeavours, which I crave leave to assure your Lordship have been very earnest and indefatigable. I pray your Lordship to make the Society sensible of my misfortune in being sent to such a wretched place and excite them to consider me whilst here, and either provide better for me, remove me to a Christian country, or else call me home."[60] John Lang writes, in a letter for which it is difficult to find a parallel even among such moving correspondents as the eighteenth-century Americans: "The same miserable state of health which at first induced me to trouble your Lordship with a supplication to be provided in bread in England still presses me to put your Lordship in mind of my misery. I have no choice left but to waste away and die here, and so leave a poor family, wretched and in want or return to England. I hope with God's assistance to remove to England next summer (if please God I live till then) and cast myself on the pity of your Lordship and other charitable

---

58. Pascoe, p. 850. The writ "about burning a heretic," issued when the sovereign decided to burn someone for heresy.
59. The extreme southwest coast of the Indian peninsula. The attention of the S.P.G. had been turned toward the possibility of Indian missionary activity at this time by the Danish Lutheran missionaries' reports.
60. John Urmston, North Carolina, Box /36, 21st, Jan. 1711/12.

persons and then, if I perish, I perish. The merciful Providence that took care of a company of pitiful lepers at the gate of Samaria will watch over me."[61] It might be truly said of the missionaries (as of many parsons at home too, of course) that the word *charity* was never out of their mouths, in one connection or another. It is a little difficult to see how Lang could have recovered his health better in England than in the colonies. True, there were more doctors in England, and probably better ones, but he has already remarked that he has no money, without which there was no physic in those days. If it were a change of climate that he wanted, surely he could, just as well, have gone north to another colony? It is difficult to avoid the idea that the parson is using his difficulties (some of which may have admittedly existed) as a lever to move the Bishop to some tangible expression of compassion. In a previous letter he had remarked that he hoped to recover his health in England, and added: "Did not my sickness oblige me to supplicate relief, I'd never desire to depart out of this corner, where there's so great need of Gospel ministers, or were I only a single man, who had no charge but myself, I'd not scruple to spend my few days here, and die in Maryland as soon as in England. But the thoughts of leaving a virtuous wife and good children here to the mercy of a people who begrudge ministers the small allowance of subsistence must be very shocking to any tender husband or parent."[62] Here Lang is being unjust to his parishioners, whatever their faults, and they had many; frontier communities would not let women and children starve to death. On the other hand, the fate of a widow and her children left friendless in

---

61. Maryland Box / 72, John Lang, Maryland, St. James parish, Annarundel County, November 22nd, 1735.
62. Maryland Box / 16. John Lang, rector of St. Luke's parish in Queen Anne's County, on Chester River in Maryland. 14th, August 1731.

London, or any of the seaports of the time is something about which it is better not to think. All that has been said hitherto need not suggest that the missionaries did not have money troubles and get into debt; we know that they did. A governor wrote to the Bishop, telling him of one "parson's progress," to poverty, in the following terms. "The late reverend Mr. John Vicary, who was sent over by your Lordship's predecessor to take charge of this church[63] was certainly a very ingenious preacher, and gave a general satisfaction to the people in the exercise of every part of his sacred office. But the duty being large and his natural constitution of body very weak and consumptive, a certain peevishness of temper mixed with a good deal of vanity so increased upon him that in a short time after his arrival he was pleased to value himself exceedingly upon the influence he had amongst the people to turn me out of the vestry, and although at that time he appeared anxious of all opportunity to affront me as he thought, both in and out of the pulpit, yet I took no manner of notice thereof but punctually went to church every Sunday, and also continued my usual contribution every six months towards the minister's support and it is an undeniable truth that Mr. Vicary's income while he remained here never amounted to less than three hundred pound per annum, and often considerably more. But the gentleman having no economy in the management of his private affairs, and being very industrious at a great expense to keep up a popularity independent of the powers of government, he at last became miserably involved in debt, which increased his bodily distemper, obliged him to return to England, and I verily believe, was the principal occasion of his death."[64]

63. Christ Church? Philadelphia.
64. 9/61.

Parsons have never been remarkable for their ability to manage their own financial affairs, as Anglican records from the Reformation downwards show. They must have felt somewhat at a loss in a land of shrewd traders and even shrewder Royal Officials, such as the Governor who met one missionary as he landed, borrowed about a year's salary from him, on the plea of some temporary need, and then refused to pay it back. This competitive spirit nearly got Parson Eversfield into a good deal of trouble. He, it will be remembered, had bought Giles Rainsford's land and goods, and gave him something above market price for them. "Your predecessor's commissary," he told the Bishop, "for no other reason than my giving him for his effects somewhat more than a common planter, who allows nothing for the buildings on the premises, neither will give for goods half the value of them, especially when a man is driven to the pinch, as Mr. Rainsford was [accused me of simony], I judge their proceedings no rule for another to walk by, and that their taking the advantage of their neighbours was no argument for my doing the like. But Mr. Henderson, having very grossly abused me in his house a little before for insisting on a couple of books he promised me, was resolved to be revenged of me, and made use of the innocent word before mentioned as a handle to keep me out of the living."[65] Elsewhere he said, "The reverend Mr. Rainsford was pleased upon Dr. Bray's recommendation to resign me his living. He had effects in these parts which I bought of him, an inventory of which I have sent your Lordship. I have been falsely charged with simony by Mr. Henderson, your predecessor's commissary."[66]

65. 21/119. John Eversfield.
66. Simony consisted in two people's making an illegal pact for a piece of ecclesiastical preferment, in this case in Eversfield's buying Rainsford's goods as an inducement to him to resign the living in his favor.

In all these complaints there is, I think, no more to be found than that the Bishop, like other eighteenth-century bishops, encouraged begging letter writers, if he did not encourage other kinds of writing. Swift, that scourge of the clergy of his age, would have enquired sardonically if the southern ministers were not enjoying the ultimate felicity of parsons on this earth, with an unlimited store of stipend tobacco for their churchwarden pipes, and an unlimited supply of rum (bartered for the stipend oats) for their punch bowls.

Next to the need for getting a good, regular stipend paid by their parishioners, the thing that most ministers were concerned about was the size of their parishes. It was a lucky missionary who could report his parish as being "four miles long and one hundred and thirty families."[67] A much more usual reply to the query, "How big is your parish?" was "About twenty-four miles long and in some places twelve broad. The exact number is not yet known till ye boundaries are better settled,"[68] or "thirty miles in length and near ten in breadth, the number of families near two hundred and twenty."[69] "My parish," remarked the incumbent of St. Pauls, Queen Anne's County, Maryland, "Is in extent about forty miles and in breadth near twenty miles, and contains in it five hundred and fifty two families."[70] Summing up his description of his living, another parson described it as: "A frontier parish, about seventy miles, inhabited, the breadth about four miles, for the lower, fifteen miles, ten miles in breadth, the next twenty four miles and about twenty miles in breadth for the residue. About twelve hundred taxeables and near four hundred families."[71] It is needless to say that

67. 25/6. St. Annes, Annapolis, Maryland.
68. 25/11. Shrewsbury Parish in Kent County, Maryland, June 1st, 1724.
69. 25/14. St. Paul's Parish, Prince George County, Maryland.
70. 25/19. St. Pauls in Queen Anne's County, Maryland.
71. 25/23. King George's parish in Prince George's county on the Potomack river, Maryland, Annapolis, May 28th, 1724.

these parishes were far larger than anything the missionaries could have known in Great Britain, where the parishes, having been laid down in medieval times, bore no relation to the contemporary distribution of population, and where moreover the number of noncomers to church was much more noticeable than in America. Thus an English parson might be lucky enough to have a church whose surrounding village had disappeared in the Middle Ages, when the parishioners were wiped out by the Black Death, for example, or he might have a church in London that attracted a very small congregation because the parish was either in a strong Calvinist neighborhood such as Spitalfields, where the foreign refugees lived, or he might have been given an Irish cure, like Swift, whose parishioners remained devout Catholics and refused to come to the established church, so that his congregation was composed of himself and the parish clerk. None of these conditions was likely to be present in the colonies, where the Anglican parishes had been calculated on the number of Church of England members, and where there was likely to be at least a small, if scattered, congregation, every member of which would expect a visit, if only because he was taxed regularly for the support of his minister. Not surprisingly, a really efficient parson was compelled to be always in his saddle or carrying litter. "The extent of our parishes," wrote the Maryland clergy to the Bishop, "is generally very large, some of them being above twenty, some thirty miles in length; by reason of the inhabitants of this country having (many of them) vast tracts of land [which] lie at least a mile asunder from their next neighbours. This large extent of parishes obligeth us to keep one, or sometimes two horses to ride on. The charges of our board and keeping our horses takes up one fourth of our greatest incomes, and the remaining three parts (considering the rates we pay for English goods in the stores, will hardly [supply] us with clothes and other necessaries, so that should some of us that have wives in England send for them and go to house keeping, we could not tell how to maintain them. There not yet being provided any minister house and glebe." A minister who fell ill so that he could not ride, and had not the means of being carried around his parish, might reckon to be almost completely cut off from the greater part of his flock. "I have for these seven years past," wrote a clergyman so situated, "laboured under such heavy sickness and bodily affliction that great part of my time has been spent in sorrow and pain at home. Now I'm hardy able to ride abroad at all. My constitution and bodily strength is so much broken that I can bear neither cold, heat, nor fatigue. There's no assistance to be had, for other clergymen have generally large parishes of their own to attend. I had for about six years a very large parish (about fifty miles in length and thirty miles in wideness) in which were three different places of worship, some of which were twelve, others eighteen miles distant from (each) other."[72]

"I am obliged every Lord's Day," wrote Christopher Wilkinson, "to preach at two churches seven miles distant, and one of those churches seventeen miles distant from my house." Parson Holt told the Bishop that "this parish is but little short of sixty miles in length, and very hilly. One Lord's Day I must ride about fourteen miles, the next about twenty four."[73] These large parishes, and the labor they entailed, probably brought about the deaths of many more missionaries than those few whose end can be put down directly to travel, such as John Garzie, in North Carolina, who was thrown from his horse, and Thomas Jenkins (whom Pascoe, with his usual ready insight, describes as "a

72. 3/52.
73. 25/89.

Welshman,") who died "of a calenture caused by the mosquitoes."[74]

Appropriately for an area that was to produce so much good horseflesh in the future, it was to riding that the south owed what religion the missionaries brought to her. North or south, travel was dangerous as well as a hardship. The clergymen's paths of peace criss-crossed with the war paths of the Indian war bands; some of them, as we shall see, narrowly evaded capture or death while engaged in their parish visiting. Mr. Browne, missionary at Portsmouth, New Hampshire, congratulates himself on the fact that "the success of his Majesty's arms has freed them from the incursions of the Indians and the frontier parts of the country may be visited with the utmost security."[75]

The sea, America's principal highway, was no less dangerous than was the land. "In our journey to New York," said a missionary, "where we were going, as we mentioned in our letter, to attend the stated annual meeting of the Corporation For The Relief Of Clergymen's Widows And Children, the first Tuesday of this month, the weather proved so stormy the day before and the day of meeting also that the members expected could not pass the Bay of New York, by which accident we could not make a majority."[76] "Besides the distance," says Parson Holt, speaking here of Maryland, "there is a great uncertainty of crossing this great and dangerous bay, in which many people perish by sudden gusts and often we must wait many days at public houses for a fit season to venture upon the water."[77] There is no use in saying that any Maryland parson was probably glad to be

74. Pascoe, pp. 852.
75. L.P.L. 1124/1.
76. 9/44.
77. 21/86. A.W. Holt, May 23rd, 1735. St. Luke's parish in Queen Anne County, on Chester River in Maryland.

kept waiting at a public house (that is, a tavern), for this particular one, Holt, was obviously one of the better sort of missionaries. He has no complaints about his cure, nor anything to say against his colleagues; just the reverse, in fact. "There are some worthy good clergy in this district. I know not the parish in all America that (if void) I should desire to exchange this for which I now enjoy. It is believed the seat of government will remove to Chester, a new town, about four miles from my house. It is the most improving town and most capable to be improved of any place in the province."[78] All the dangers and discomforts of parishional travel applied manyfold to the necessary journeys made to synods or assemblies of the clergy such as have been described above. More about the dangers of synodal traveling will be said in a moment, but we must notice there that, although the parishes of the missionaries were big, the proposal (in Maryland) to reduce them and the parsons' salaries proportionately did not meet with approval. A minister complained that "our assembly are now at last resolved not only to lessen our revenues but also to divide several (if not all) our parishes, which will make our maintenance so mean and contemptible that it will both starve us and discourage others."[79] The dangers of riding to synod were so considerable that there was an important constitutional effect felt in the inability of the missionaries to come together, discuss their grievances, and concert action. To the end, the Church of England parsons remained scattered, unvocal, and at a disadvantage when in conflict with better organized church groups. The trouble involved in canvassing the opinions of one's colleagues is touched on by Alexander Adams. "I designed to have visited most of

78. *Ibid.*
79. 21/166.

the clergy of Maryland to subscribe the enclosed, but we have had such a dry hot sultry summer, such as I cant remember the like, that I could not undertake it, and this time I have had a slow fever and dare not be so long from home, for it would be five hundred miles riding at least. Those that have subscribed took me above fifty miles."[80] There was another reason why ministers could not well leave home for long; they were expected to act as hosts to the travelers who stopped to stable their horses and stretch their legs at the parsonage. "I think indeed our parishes are too large," said a minister, "but unless they can proportionately advance the price and value of the remaining tobacco to what they deduct from it we must necessarily use some other endeavours for the support of our families, besides we are so much burdened with the entertainment of travellers through the want of convenient houses for that purpose that a better maintenance than we have at present will not be sufficient to allow them hospitality. I for my part have been obliged to lodge and provide for man and horse at least three nights a week ever since March last."[81]

If stipends and the size of parishes often brought a sigh to the lips of incumbents, the parish churches and their contents must have reconciled them to much of the hardship and deprivation they encountered. If it was a great comfort to have with one, in the parsonage, some of the material luxury of the age, it was even better to see rising at the end of the glebe a worthy house of God. The eighteenth century has often been criticized on account of its Laodicean lukewarmness, but it was the last period that produced buildings that revealed themselves, at first glance, the house of a spirit, and not merely an edifice devoted to ecclesiastical

80. 3/161.
81. 21/66.

purposes. Many of these beautiful colonial churches remain, the proper pride of their congregations and communities; others have been lovingly restored; some have
gone completely. The accounts of the missionaries are of
interest for the imaginary reconstruction of the latter and
also because they show how parsons (especially the first
ones in a parish) set about providing for the building of a
fitting place of worship. Not only the parson, but the parish
as well, thought very highly of their church. If the provincials were sometimes slow in paying their minister, they
never hung back in providing money or labor for the
church. "Our parish church," said the incumbent of St.
Michaels, Talbot County, "has cost us several times more
than five hundred pounds. We have a new chapel in building on which there [is] already laid out half above two
hundred lb."[82] Jacob Henderson remarked that he had
"but one cure, a church and chapel. The chapel begun by
my wife at her own expense, and since finished by me for
the use of an extreme part of the parish, well and decently
beautified."[83] "I got built," a missionary told the Bishop, "a
very handsome brick church, seventy seven feet in length,
thirty five feet in wideness, and twenty two feet pitch in the
walls, all plastered and whitewashed in the inside, furnished
with a very decent chancel, communion table, and rails,
pulpit, reading desk, clerk's pew and four rows of pews
from end to end, a large gallery in one end from side to side
for common people and servants. The church [is] well
lighted, having thirteen windows, ten feet in height each,
three doors and a bell of about a hundred and seventy
pound weight. And in forwarding this good work I sunk
above a hundred pound sterling of my own money."[84]

82. 25/15. St. Michael's Parish, Talbot County, Maryland.
83. 25/84.
84. 25/47. John Laing, St. James parish, Maryland, May 29th, 1735. He refers
here to a former parish.

Sometimes the colonials, reduced to their shirts and petticoats by a surprise Indian raid, were too poor to begin a church, even with the assistance of their missionary. Recourse was had on these occasions to the Bishop. "By this packet,"[85] wrote Nathaniel Cotton from Florida, "his honour the Lieutenant Governor will forward to Lord Hillsborough a duplicate of the dutiful petition of the inhabitants of this province to the King, setting forth their great want of a church, and their present inability to build one, and humbly pray that Government will assist them with a grant of a thousand or one thousand five hundred pounds, to enable them to build a church and glebe house. I regret saying that the only church built in this province since its cession was completed by our Roman Catholic subjects at Mobile."[86] Such was the enthusiasm shown by many parishes that they had erected a church before any minister had reached them. The churchwardens of St. Helena, Granville County, South Carolina, told the Bishop that "Through the misfortune of an Indian war we have been without the blessing of having either church or minister. Now we have a handsome brick church, a building which will be finished in three months. Our humble petition to your Lordship is that your Lordship will be pleased to send us a sober and learned parson to be our minister, we being a frontier parish."[87] The industrious frontiersman of the day could turn his hand to anything, even building church furniture. "The people have likewise made a number of pews in the church," wrote Parson Palmer, "which seem to fill apace."[88]

Even more regrettable than the lost churches, in some

---

85. I.e., mailboat.
86. Florida Box /83. Pensacola, December 15th, 1768.
87. 10/68. Petition from the churchwardens of St. Helena, Granville County, South Carolina.
88. L.P.L. 1124/2/232.

ways, are the plate and church ornaments of the time, more of which, proportionately, has been destroyed than actual church architecture. Many of the altar vessels must have been the work of the early American silversmith, who seemed to draw new inspiration from the native silver in which he worked, and the missionaries letters are full of mouthwatering references to them. Many churches were, of course, not lucky enough to possess communion plate. "With great regret of mind," wrote Thomas Thomson, of Dorchester, Maryland, to the Bishop, "I declare that as yet my parishioners have not yet been prevailed with to provide necessaries for the decent performance of divine service, having neither surplice, pulpit, cloth, nor linen, or vessels for the communion table. But there is of late something of a fund beginning for these holy uses."[89] Another incumbent remarked: "I have a good large bible and common prayer book, but neither surplice, pulpit cloth, cushion, nor plate for the communion service but pewter."[90] Even colonial or Georgian pewter is much preferable to most of the gold or silver communion vessels produced nowadays, but it seems that not many churches merely had pewter and nothing else. Many incumbents could remark, with just gratification: "The service plate at the communion table cost 30lb. Our pulpit and communion table are decently adorned with blue cloth and good linen."[91] The completely furnished church was often the result of the cooperation of many. That of which Christopher Wilkinson was incumbent is a good example. "I am further pressed upon by my parishioners," he wrote to the Bishop "(who are now building a new brick church, and the best in the province) hum-

89. 25/. Thomas Thomson, Dorchester, Maryland.
90. 25/2. St. Paul's parish, Baltimore, Maryland.
91. 25/15. St. Michaels Parish, Talbot County, Maryland.

bly to entreat your Lordship to contribute some plate for the altar. We hope to receive ornaments for the pulpit and the altar table by some merchants trading from Leverpoole in our parts. We want a bible and common prayer book also."[92]

Those colonists to whom the missionaries had gone out to minister seem to have responded very gratifyingly to their services. Many of them had, of course, been for years without the church service to which they had become accustomed in their youth, and they, as well as their unbaptized and unconfirmed children were delighted to see the newcomers. A great deal in the parsons' letters home must of course be put down to self-congratulation, self-deception, and a desire to impress the Bishop. Many of the congregation "members" that are claimed were probably temporary incomers from other congregations, or from those who normally did go to church but were sampling the new ministers' sermons. Many must have gone to see a parson for the same reason that they would have gone to see a traveling menagerie; they had never seen anything like one before. With all these reservations made, however, there was a good deal of solid achievement on the part of the missionaries. "Such is the general good disposition of the people in this province," wrote a missionary from Maryland, "that where there are exemplary and diligent clergymen, there wants not success."[93] "As for our parishes," wrote another, "most of us say we have very few dissenters, and that our churches are well filled and that a manifest reformation is wrought in the whole course of the lives of the inhabitants of this country within these twenty or thirty years past, conspicuous as the sun at noon day and freely

92. 3?/191. July 29th, 1719. Christopher Wilkinson.
93. 25/85. Talbot County, Maryland, September 27th, 173.

owned by all that have lived any time here."[94] The following letters, announcing a successful conversion tour, are typical of many.

"I went up into the country and agreed with the vestry of Northwest Parish in Albemarle County for ten months, reserving two months for visiting the other parts of the country. They were to pay me £400 of their currency (which at ten for one is not a par with sterling (and I have not received fifty).

"The parish I live in is of a vast extent, being upwards of one hundred miles in length and fifty in breadth. I preach in seven different places, which obliges me to ride every month two hundred and sixty miles. I have baptized about a thousand infants and thirty adults. The first time I administered the Blessed Sacrament of the Supper I had only four communicants, the last time twenty. We are very happy in having no different sects or opinions in this part of the country, but I have great reason to complain of a Laodicean lukewarmness and immorality. But lower down in the country there are a great many Quakers and Anabaptists; in my last journey I had a great many of them my auditors and I baptized five adults that formerly professed Quakerism, and I believe, were there a minister settled among them, they would mostly come over to the church and a better way of thinking."[95]

"Mr. Granville is now on a progress in which he will baptize some hundreds. We hear Mr. Granville will leave us when his year is expired, unless your Lordship with the Society think proper to establish a missionary in this province."

94. Maryland Box /19, Oxford, Maryland, July 16th, 1724.
95. North Carolina Box /25. John Boyd, Northwest Parish, North Carolina, April 12th, 1735.

"Doctor Marsden officiates gratis at a place called Onslow, forty miles from his own habitation, and a clergyman beneficed in Virginia preaches once in a month in a precinct named Bertie. Mr. Gale, who came from England lately, brought a copy of complaints against me to his Sacred Majesty by William Smith, he knows these complaints to be false."[96]

Another Maryland clergyman commented: "My congregations are much larger than my two churches can hold, so that the people are obliged to crowd at the outsides of the doors and windows. They seem very joyful to have the public service of the church once again performed against them on the Lord's Day." "Every Sunday and the most noted Holy Days," wrote a missionary, "there is commonly a large congregation."

A new incumbent acted as a nucleus around which a church could gather. Every parish contained a number of backsliding Anglicans who had neglected their church and either gone to hear ministers of other denominations or stayed away from church altogether. It was a missionary's first task to reclaim these lapsed church members, and usually it was not too difficult a business to do so. "It pleased God," said an incumbent, "to prosper my labours with visible success. I had no more than eleven communicants when I entered upon the cure, and when I took my leave there were eighty five, all belonging to this parish."[97] "Before the twenty eighth of June last," wrote a missionary, "I have baptised five hundred and ten grown persons and children, and, since, forty five children, and three adults."[98] The missionaries reported that not only did they gather in the scattered congregations, but they also made many converts

96. 10/27. George Burrington, May 10th, 1732.
97. 25/52.
98. 9/93.

in the Presbyterian, Swedish, and German churches. Nathaniel Cotton wrote from Pensacola to say that he was preaching to a congregation largely composed of Presbyterians.[99] The church at "Apoquiniminek" was "very populous and consists not only of English but also many Dutch, as from Bohemia in Maryland, who are very desirous to hear the gospel preached in English."[100] The incumbent of St. Michaels mentions that he had baptized "of Quaker families a great many,"[101] and the vestrymen of Christ's Church in Philadelphia testified that Mr. Peters, their minister, "has drawn great numbers of the more understanding dissenters of all persuasions;" the Mayor of Philadelphia witnessed that the vestrymen "are men of the best characters, circumstances, credit, and reputation and well beloved and esteemed in this city," attaching the mayoral seal to their statement to attest the truth of what he said.

It was hoped by the missionaries that the Lutherans and moderate Calvinists, whose ideas on religion approximated more closely to the Church of England than those of the Quakers, for example, might be persuaded to become Anglicans. The frequent neglect of the home government of Swedes and Gemans to supply them with ministers led many of them to do so, as the incumbent of Oxford points out in the following letter: "I acknowledge your Lordship's goodness in countenancing the request of the people of Oxford for my continuance among them. It is of some use to my large family, and no inconvenience, but rather a pleasure to me to ride out among them on Sundays and other leisure days. In summer I have a country house for my family within two miles of where the former missionary

99. Florida Box /83. December 15th, 1768.
100. 9/88.
101. 25/15. St. Michaels Parish, Talbot County, Maryland.

resided, and my attendance then is very convenient, as I am then as near Oxford Church as to Philadelphia, being five miles from each. The mission flourishes greatly, and has the addition of most of the Swedish families that belonged to a congregation near it. They have become communicants at Oxford, and we are building another church in the mission five miles from the present one, for the convenience of these old Swedish families chiefly. The people have earnestly requested me not to leave them yet, and were under some apprehensions that one of the young gentlemen I recommended in my last to your Lordship, viz. Mr. Hopkinson, a distant relation of the Bishop of Worcester, was to apply for that mission. He is a worthy good lad, but has a sort of impediment in his speech, which the people of Oxford did not like, and there are other reasons that would make that an unfit place for him, even if he wanted it, which I cannot think he does. For it is one of the poorest missions in our province, with a very difficult people, who would not willing receive any person put upon them without their previous knowledge." The writer had been in the colonies too long if anything he said was likely to carry more weight, in London, than the plea of a relative of the Bishop of Worcester, however distant, however impeded.[102]

The German church corresponded with the Bishop, and it will be seen later that whole families even of first-generation German colonists, who had no doubt come out as indentured servants, had become Anglicans, in full communion with the church and going to the missionaries to be married. Mr. Barton of Cumberland County, Pennsylvania, reported confidently that the German Lutherans had asked, in their *coetus*, for a union with the Church of England, and that the Dutch Calvinists had

102. 9/42. Philadelphia, May 3rd, 1771.

drawn up constitutions obliging themselves to conform to
the canons and constitutions of the established church.[103]
All in all, however, neither the Germans nor the Dutch
fulfilled the promise that they had had for the Anglicans,
and their final separation from the Anglican viewpoint is
perhaps best symbolized by the German Lutheran pastor,
who, at the Revolution, preached a sermon on the text
"There is a time for all things," and at the end of it, stripped
off gown and bands to reveal a colonel's uniform under-
neath, remarking as he did so: "Now is the time to fight."[104]

One of the reasons for the presence of the parsons in
America was the conversion of the heathen, but it was no
easy task. A question in the printed form sent to missionaries and which they filled in during 1724 was: "Are
there any infidels, bond or free within your parish, and
what means are used for their conversion?"[105] The answers
made to this varied very much, but on the whole they
showed that the clergymen had a proper sense of responsi-
bility toward those members of the community who, imported wholesale from the West Coast of Africa, were still
uninstructed in the Christian faith and followed in America
the peculiar worship of their forefathers. At home, there
was a great deal of enthusiasm in the Society for the conversion of the Negroes, and Bishop Fleetwood of St. Asaph
preached a sermon called "An address to serious Christians
among ourselves to assist the society for propagating the
Gospel in carrying on the work of instructing the negroes in
our plantations abroad,"[106] which was distributed by the
missionaries to slave owners with great effect.[107] The par-

---

103. Pascoe, p. 97.
104. Sweet, p. 265.
105. 25/1.
106. Pascoe, p. 8.
107. *Ibid*.

sons often had great difficulty, as will be seen, in persuading
the planters to let their slaves be baptized, either because
they objected on racial grounds, or because they thought
that baptism would free the slaves and that "a christen'd
slave is by law free."[108] No one seems to have put forward an
explanation of this curious and quite false belief, but it is
possible to explain it by the fact that some of the planters in
the south, if they came from England, may have been captured and enslaved by the Barbary Corsairs, or have known
people who were slaves of theirs at one time. The North
African pirates continued to be a thorn in the flesh of
persons sailing to America, and of the growing American
commerce fleet until 1816, when they were virtually destroyed by the allied fleets in an action that was also the last
great day of Nelson's Navy. Among the pirate communities
a man was only reckoned to be a slave until he had mastered
the first chapter of the Koran, which released him. This
religious act, the first step in becoming a Muslim as baptism
was the first step in becoming a Christian, removed servile
status. The missionaries comment on the unwillingness of
some slave owners to have their slaves baptized, or for them
to be confirmed afterwards,[109] but it was probably misun-
derstood and misrepresented by them. For some time at
least, many of the confirmed Negroes may have continued
in the exercise of their old religion, those African rites
whose seeming psychic effectiveness puzzled, while it repel-
led, white observers on the coast. Thus while the "young
gent," who resolved "never to come to the holy table while
slaves are received there,"[110] may have objected to the Negroes as Negroes, he might, as a good churchman, dislike
the idea of taking communion with those who had lately

108. *Ibid*.
109. Pascoe, p. 15.
110. *Ibid*.

perhaps, sipped at a Voodoo chalice filled with rum, gunpowder, grave dirt, and human blood. This difficulty of reconciling the nominal official religion of native peoples who worked for the British settlers and their private and real religion was one that was to continue to the end of the British colonial period, and the author remembers being told, by a New Zealand lady, how annoyed her grandmother was when she found that the Maori servants, whom she had led in family worship every morning, sometimes slipped off, at the weekends, to attend a ritual cannibal feast. The missionaries, who were not perhaps great students of comparative religion, do not seem to have seen the force of the African religion, though they reluctantly admitted the hold it had over some of their parishioners. It is against this situation that the many S.P.G. records of baptisms must be set. In the great majority of cases there was probably little point in baptizing any of the slaves at all, since, apart from those slaves whom the planters had instructed, many of them must still have been attached to their own religion.

One missionary reported that there were "some heathen slaves, instructed by their masters and him, and baptised after due examination."[111] Another, John Donaldson, noted that in his parish of King and Queen, St. Mary's and Charles county, "negroes and mulattoes, some of them that understand English, come duly to church where the means of instruction are to be had."[112] Evidently Voodoo had a hold on even the second-generation Africans, a fact confirmed by the remark of William Tibbs, rector of St. Pauls, Baltimore, who says that "many of them [Negroes and mulattoes] I have baptised and instructed in the principles

111. 25/6.
112. 25/25. John Donaldson, King and Queen parish, St. Marys and Charles county.

of ye Christian Religion, but most have refused instruction."[113] "I baptised some of their negroes," wrote Rainsford from Chowan, "though with much difficulty I obtained the leave for so doing from their masters."[114] One of the amiable habits of the compilers of questionnaires, which has not disappeared with the eighteenth century, is to ask for information they should already have from other sources. Hence, although the Bishop kept a separate file about the conversion of negroe slaves, he had to be reminded respectfully by the incumbent of St. Michaels of the fact in the following words. "What infidels? There are negroe slaves, and what means are used for their conversion your Lordship will know by our general letter. However I have baptised several."[115]

Many of the planters took the conversion and religious instruction of their slaves very seriously and treated religion with much more thoroughness than was shown by the employers of free factory hands in England, hands who were certainly not less heathen than the Africans. An S.P.G. missionary mentioned two South Carolina ladies, Madam Edwards and Madam Haigue, who had been particularly active in this respect.[116] One planter even employed a religious instructor for his slaves, really extraordinary solicitude when it is remembered how few parsons there were in America. "Mr. Winter," wrote the planter, "has been employed as a catechist to the negroes belonging to the estate or plantation of my aforesaid predecessor, for these twelve months, and has for this time behaved in a sober decent manner, and as I apprehend consistent with his profession as a Christian and in the capacity he has been

113. 25/2. St. Pauls Parish, Baltimore, Maryland, William Tibbs.
114. 10/38. Chowan in North Carolina, July 25th, 1712.
115. 25/15. St. Michaels parish, Talbot county, Maryland.
116. Pascoe, p. 16.

acting as well as human infirmities will permit."[117] Not all planters were as serious minded as this one, and sometimes one gets the impression that they sympathised with their slaves' attachment to their ancestral religion and did not want them baptized because they felt forced baptism and attendance at church might unsettle them, or because they thought it better that slaves after work should employ themselves at the *hounfort* rather than plot rebellion against their masters. "There are negroe slaves," said James Robertson, "whereof some come to church and are baptised and others who neither by their own consent nor their masters are willing to be baptised." At a visitation held at Oxford, Mr. Fletcher said that his parishioners "were generally so brutish that they would not suffer their negroes to be instructed, catechised, or baptised."[118] This tendency on the part of masters was of course reprobated by the parsons. "I often in my sermons," remarked a clergyman, "press the necessity of their instruction. I catechise them in church and out of church, and have baptised great numbers of them. Their issue are baptised when infants."[119]

The Bishop, who liked arranging things into categories, had divided the infidels for the purposes of reports about them, into "bond" and "free," which meant, usually, into Negroes and Indians, although there seem to have been a good many Indian slaves, bought from their fellow countrymen, among the Africans. The presence of these Indians on the plantations allowed the first missionaries to get to know them, and attempt their conversion under the best possible conditions; this is notably the case in Mr. Thomas's ministering to the Indian slaves in South Carolina, "who in

---

117. Georgia Box /118. Request for orders from Samuel Frink in Savannah in Georgia, December 7th, 1770.
118. 21/110. June 16th, 1731.
119. 25/184.

the Cooper River district alone outnumbered the savage Yammonsees."[120] It was, nevertheless to these "wild Indians" that Thomas had been destined as a missionary, and he had even been given a grant of £10 to "be laid out in stuffs for the use of the wild Indians." This sum, judiciously spent on paint, knives, stockings, mirrors, and the other commodities with which white negotiators were wont to tempt the red men, ought to have won at least a hearing from the Yammonsees for Thomas, but he never seems to have gone near a free Yammonsee at all. Instead, he wrote home to say that they had revolted from the Spaniards because they would not be Christians, were in so much danger of invasion that they were not at leisure to attend to instruction, nor was it safe to venture among them.[121] Thomas then set about the more congenial task of ministering to the white settlers and their slaves. This tame beginning was carried on by the South Carolina parsons who followed Thomas, and other clergymen did not hesitate to write home, pointing out, with much show of reason, that many of the settlers needed their ministration more than the Indians because they were "worse than heathen," and that the great obstacle to the natives being converted was the scandalous lives of the professing Christians in the colony. The Society achieved one of its favorite and spectacular pieces of missionary work by the conversion of "a Yammonsee prince, at the request of his father and of the Emperor of the Indians,"[122] whoever he may have been. Great parade was made on this occasion, the boy being baptized in the Royal Chapel of Somerset House on Quinquagesima Sunday, 1715, with Lord Carteret one of the

---

120. Pascoe, p. 12.
121. *Ibid*.
122. Pascoe, p. 17.

proprietors of South Carolina, as a sponsor, and presented to King George I afterwards.[123] Spectacular "conversions" of this sort, including presentation at court, were very popular with the Society. They culminated, though they did not end, in the visit of five Mohawk chiefs to England in 1710.[124] It is doubtful whether any of these court masquerades gave any solid impetus toward the conversion of the Indians, though they may have looked well in the newspapers. Did the S.P.G. really believe that there was an "Emperor of the Yammonsees," or an "Emperor of the Cherequois" (Cherokees) as its emissaries reported?[125] If it was really ignorant that these high-sounding titles conveyed very little, any experienced frontier trader would have enlightened it. So, for that matter, would a reading of the Jesuit "Relations" of missionary work in Canada. The fatuity of this policy of conversion of Indian "royalty" is well illustrated in the present case. So far from being a help in the Christianization of his people, the "prince" wrote back from Charleston (which was as far as he dared penetrate into Indian territory) to say that his father, the King, and all his friends were missing, prisoners in a fight with neighbouring tribesmen. In the same year news reached the Society that another "son of the Emperor of the Yammonsees" was being brought up as a Christian.[126] This was presumably the son of another "Emperor," the title, with the sketchy powers it conferred, having passed to some more active warrior.

It is difficult to imagine a Celtic missionary reporting to Aidan or St. Cuthbert that the heathen English were "not at

123. *Ibid*.
124. Carson I.A. Ritchie, *The New World*, (Westminster: Church Information Board, 1957).
125. Pascoe, p. 17.
126. *Ibid*.

leisure to attend to instruction," that "they would not be Christians," and that it was not "safe to venture among them," so that it would be better to minister, not to the heathen, but to the Christians of Galloway, who might set the natives a bad example, or who might become "worse than the heathen themselves." It is, on the other hand, not difficult to imagine the flea in the ear that anyone would have got, if they had dared to do so. These were different days. The Society accepted, apparently without a murmur, the submission of Mr. Thomas and his fellow workers that it was too dangerous for them to do what they had been sent from England to accomplish. In 1715 there was a general uprising of the Indians from Cape Fear to St. Augustine, in which the Appalachis, Calabaws, Creeks, and Yammonsees wiped out a British garrison and wrought untold havoc on the settlers. Hundreds died because the missionaries had failed in their duty. A more vigorous evangelization policy might have nipped the Indian war in the bud; it would have certainly have provided a buffer party of "friendly" Indians who could have persuaded their compatriots to lay down the hatchet, or have given warning of the approach of raiding parties. The surprise of Port Royal and St. Bartholomews need not have been so complete as it was.[127]

The missionary record among the Indians in other states was not so bad as that in South Carolina. Mr. Rainsford, whom we have met already, at least made many attempts to convert the Chowans, who were, however, not hostile.[128] Samuel Frink, whose testimonial from the planter on whose estate he had been employed as a catechist to the Negroes, we have already noticed, made some efforts at converting the Chickasaws, in Georgia, without much success, how-

127. Pascoe, chap. 3.
128. *Ibid.*, chap. 4.

ever. Neither were the activities of the missionaries in Pennsylvania very prosperous in this respect, though the heroic Mr. Barton of Cumberland county, whose congregation came to church on Sunday with their muskets over their shoulders, vowing that they would "die Protestants and freemen sooner than live idolaters and slaves," and who frequently led his parishioners against the combined attacks of the French and Indians, was, not surprisingly, respected by the savages, who occasionally attended his church.[129] When the Society agreed to spend the large sum of £100 a year on training native Indians as missionaries to their fellow countrymen instead of sending white parsons to them, it was virtually admitting defeat. New England missionary activities to the Indians were well intentioned but not very successful, with the exception of the mission to the Mohawks. In the north, too, the Anglicans had to encounter, not merely an aversion from the white man's religion, but the powerful counterattraction of the Gospel as preached by the French missionaries in Canada.

Altogether, Anglican missions to the Indians during this period were not nearly so successful as those of other denominations. One has only to think of the much greater impact made on the Indians by the Moravians, or the Presbyterians, or the Jesuits.[130] Significantly, the missionaries numbered no martyrs in their ranks during the missions to the Indians, as against the numerous ones to be found in the Jesuit and Moravian missionaries. All this is not to decry the personal courage of the parsons. They were brave men, or they would never had faced an Atlantic voyage in the first place. Nor did they shrink from remaining, as many of them did, in the middle of Indian territory during wartime,

129. Pascoe, chap. 8. *Ibid.*,
130. Sweet, p. 237 and the chapter generally.

or taking musket in hand like Mr. Barton for the defense of their communities. It was rather that a successful missionary to the Indian was required to live like an Indian himself. Nor was this an easy task for anyone, least of all an eighteenth-century gentleman, who liked washing, and putting on a clean shirt. Mr. Barton remarked feelingly that "their customs and manner of living are so opposite to the genius and constitution of our people, that they could never become familiar to them."[131] The Indians never washed, neither did they wash the utensils from which they ate; they traveled a great part of the time, at too rapid a pace for European comfort; they lived in smoke-filled dwellings and ate "bears, foxes, wolves, raccoons, polecats and even snakes . . . with as much cheerfulness as Englishmen do their best beef and mutton." It was, then an element of repulsion for these "nasty" people, as much as a fear of losing their hair, that stood in the way of an Anglican drive for the conversion of the natives. When a missionary did undertake Indian work, he was careful to point out all the discomforts it entailed, and suggest that he be remunerated in accordance with these hardships. The Rev. Godfrey Delius, in a letter to the Bishop, makes just this point.[132] A cure of red souls, he suggests, is a difficult manner, which cannot be successfully be entertained by everyone who wishes it, and for that matter who does? Rather than be undervalued in his remuneration, he would prefer to return to Europe, in spite of his experience with the Indians. Delius was of course, quite right in his own way; there were great difficulties facing the missionary to the red men, particularly the linguistic ones; to a hard-headed son of the eighteenth-century church, devoid of enthusiasm, it seemed reasona-

131. Pascoe, p. 38.
132. Fulham Papers, Box 6.

ble that the laborer should have his hire. Again we have come a long way down the road from the missionaries who began the English Church, relinquishing in some cases the lives of princes that lay waiting them in the Celtic lands to come south. The failure of the parsons to begin a real drive for the conversion of the heathen is one of the tragedies of eighteenth-century America. Successful conversion might have secured the survival of many of those brave and unique nations that disappeared in the colonial period; it would at least have rendered that extinction less horrible.

Without this rather lengthy disquisition it would be difficult to understand correctly the letters in which the missionaries refer to the Indians, particularly those from Maryland. "There are Indians whose language we don't understand," reported James Robertson, under the title of "Infidels" in the Bishop's questionnaire, and that was all he had to say about them.[133] "The free" (infidels), noted the incumbent of King George's parish on the Potomack, "are native Indians who are averse to Christianity."[134] The parson of Stepney also mentioned the presence of Indians.[135] Occasionally a minister reported that there had been Indians in the parish, but that they had packed up and moved away. Thus the parson of William and Mary parish, when asked "Are there any infidels, bond or free, within your parish?" must have congratulated himself on being able to reply. "No they are removed backwards."[136] Few missionaries even attempted to make an honest reply to the second half of the question put above, which was; "And what means are used for their conversion?" They appear to

133. 25/17. Coventry Parish in Somerset County, Maryland, James Robertson.
134. 25/23. King George's parish in Prince George county on the Potomack River, Maryland. Endorsed Annapolis, May 28th, 1724.
135. 25/20. Stepney Parish, Somerset County, Maryland.
136. Fulham Papers: not assigned.

have left the red parishioners very much to themselves. Occasionally a sincere desire for Indian conversion is expressed in the letters. "I cant easily express the satisfaction I had," wrote Sir William Keith, Deputy Governor in the Province of Philadelphia, "in seeing your Lordship's letters to Colonel Spotswood in Virginia, relating to the treaties which that gentleman had concluded with the Indians, in order to educate and instruct the children of those poor infidels."[137]

It is only on occasion however, that the Bishop is reminded that the Indians are heathen waiting conversion, more usually they are heathen raging furiously. "We have been destitute of means," wrote the churchwardens of St. Thomas, Bath Town, North Carolina,[138] "ever since our first settlement, to allow a decent maintenance for a Protestant minister by reason of our poverty (to which our indigence and incapacity the late massacre or severe persecution of the savage Indian nations bordering on us have not a little contributed.)" "For some years past," wrote Mr. Hugh Bryan to a friend, [The Almighty] "hath at divers times been scourging of us, by drought, by repeated diseases on man and beast, by insurrections of our slaves, and lately by baffling shamefully our enterprise against our enemy, so as to make us a byword and a hissing among the heathen that are round about us."[139] "Since my arrival in this province," wrote Nicholas Trott to the Bishop, "it hath pleased God strangely to alter the scene of affairs here by sending one of the greatest afflictions that could well be brought upon this province. The barbarous heathen Indians that are round

---

137. 10/1. Petition to the Bishop of London from the churchwardens of St. Thomas parish, Pamphio river, North Carolina, for help in building a new church.
138. Fulham Papers, not assigned.
139. *Ibid*.

about us, from North to South, and five times our number, have all united themselves together, and made war upon us, beginning with the murder of our traders, and several of the inhabitants in the out settlements, and have since made further incursions into the settlements, killing all they meet, destroying and laying waste the plantations where they come, and plundering and then burning the houses, lying skulking in the bushes and swamps, and shooting down persons as they pass by.

"And, when our forces march against them, then they retire into woods and swamps, so that we know not where to find them, nor could follow them if we did, so that we may as well go to war with the wolfs and bears."[140]

The effect of these raids on the daily lives of the missionaries was considerable. Sometimes, like Rainsford, they had to flee before the advancing war parties and lie up in another colony for a time; sometimes, like Guy, they escaped on the last boat out of a stricken township; sometimes they were shut up in a fort beleaguered by the Indians, like Maule, and ministered to the sick and wounded.[141] One of the effects of the Indian raids was to impoverish the colonists in the territory they passed through. It is often tempting to think, fallaciously, of the frontiersmen simply moving back to their own townships, rebuilding, and going on with a minimum of discomfort. This does not seem to have been the case, in the south at least, where J. La Pierre of St. Dennis, and P. De Rich, of Santee, suffered great destitution along with their communities after South Carolina's Indian war.[142] Not unnaturally, with the dead to bury, the sick to tend, and the bereaved to comfort, along with a

140. 10/6.
141. Pascoe, p. 18.
142. *Ibid.*

rousing sermon to preach to the local militia before they
marched off, in the Cotton Mather style, some missionaries
found it difficult to find time to write back to London.

"The misery and distress of this unhappy province," remarked a parson to the Bishop, "bleeding under the mur-
derous knives of a savage enemy, instigated and led on by
Popish cruelty, have been so unspeakably great, and the
confusions arising from a Quaker government, obstinately
persevering in their absurd pacific policy, while the sword
of the enemy was at our throats, have so thoroughly en-
grossed my attention and engaged my weak endeavours to
defeat such wicked principles, and procure relief to a miserable people, that I hope to be excused for not having
sooner returned by humble acknowledgements."[143] "We
are in great danger of being destroyed by the heathen,"
remarked John Urmston, with further reference to the
Quakers, "the people being of quaking principles with reference to the maintaining of the clergy and fighting."[144]

Though not anxious to convert the Indians, the missionaries did not go out of their way to avoid them while on
the warpath either, and seem to have treated their incursions with the same stoutness that their parishioners displayed. Among the letters to the Bishop asking for permission to leave the country, or announcing the intention to
return to England, the parsons talk about ill health, dis-
agreement with parishioners, trouble with the dissenters,
inability to live on the stipend, and deranged affairs at
home, but they do not mention the savages. Indeed, most of
the parsons were probably an asset to a frontier community,
and one of them in particular, Thomas Barton of York and

143. Letter from William Smith of Philadelphia, November 7th 1756. L.P.L.
1123/II/105.
144. 10/40. John Urmston. 1712.

Cumberland counties, exhibited to a large degree the qualities of a successful militia commander, marching day and night to cut off the columns of the enemy as they approached his parishes. He deserves a statue, and doubtless would have got one had not he been unfortunate enough to take the wrong side in the unpleasantness of 1776.

3

Other Denominations

O NE of the most attractive features of the colonial
Americans was that they were Americans, and not
Catholics or Protestants first. While the British Roman
Catholic looked secretly to the exiled line of Stuart as his
lawful Kings, and the French Huguenot extended the hand
of friendship to any foreign power that would protect him,
the American colonies represent (almost for the first time, it
seems) the spectacle of a people of very diverse religious
beliefs united together. Some historians, notably Parkman,
have tried to give to the successive French and Indian wars
the character of a religious crusade, with gallant Protestants
battling against Popish cruelty, forgetting that Anne and
the Georges had no more faithful subjects than those
Catholics who in the southern colonies fought against the
Spaniards. Parkman forgets, too, that nothing would ever
have persuaded the French or Spanish to like the British in

the Americas, not even the fact that they were of the same religion as themselves. If anything, the Spaniards hated English Catholics more than they did those of other denominations. A seventeenth-century Catholic Englishman, who with a party of coreligionists was on his way out to found a colony in the West Indies, and hoped to establish friendly, or at least neutral relations with the Spaniards, bore up to a Spanish vessel he encountered, only to be received with a shout from her captain "Amayna perros!" (Strike, dogs!) and a broadside to confirm this order to surrender. After having escaped from this sea chase, the Englishman noted sadly in his journal that he saw that unwelcome as he and his friends might be at home, they would be even more unwelcome to the lords of the Indies. No Englishman, were he Catholic or Protestant, was allowed to sail in a Spanish ship to the Americas, and Thomas Gage, an English priest in Spanish service, only succeeded in reaching Guatemala by having himself hoisted on board the ship in which he and some other priests were to travel in a barrel marked "Biscuit." He did not like what he saw of the Spanish treatment of the natives, though he has the honesty to confess that that of the British was not much better, and when he returned to England, having turned to Anglicanism in the meantime, he advised Cromwell to send an expedition to help the Ancient Maya, still holding out in the middle of their swamps.[1]

This pressure from outside, then, on the British colonists had an enormous, unifying effect on people of very different religious beliefs, and in consequence there was very little of what Europeans would describe as religious persecution. What there was, in America, was so anemic as barely to deserve the term. There was, on the other hand, something that was entirely lacking in the Europe of the day, an

1. Ritchie, *The New World*.

enormous amount of goodwill between the different denominations. "They have three ways of permitting religion in this country," remarks an anonymous writer in an undated note of probably the eighteenth century: "1. They connive at all religions, whatever, unless they meddle with the Government. 2. Toleration; when their designs are made known to the Bailiff, who upon some consideration assures them, that he will not disturb them. But both these ways are precarious, and depend too much upon the arbitrary humour of that officer who may shut up the church doors without assigning any reason. 3. The last sort is an establishment from the states, which was secure against all attempts."[2]

The way in which the personal side of this mutual relation of tolerance was established is indicated in a letter in which William Smith, writing of Father Hardeing, a neighbouring priest, describes him as "A worthy Jesuit in this town, who was always on good terms with us."[3] This display of good feeling was peculiarly American, and the descendants of people like the Cordiners, who had suffered persecution (often at the hands of their fellow countrymen) in the Old World, would have seen in it the peculiar justification of the American colonies. A similar friendliness was shown by other Protestants to the Anglican parsons. One of the Bishop's Commissaries, who has been quoted above, refers, in rather surprised tones, to the welcome given him in the colony by dissenters. Yet these non-Anglicans were, some of them, great grandsons of people who had spent a large part of their lives in hiding, in exile, or in the Clink[4] because of the Bishop of London's Commissary. It was a large

2. 9/45. *Plantations, 1700.*
3. 9/229. Philadelphia, October 30th, 1773. William Smith.
4. The famous ecclesiastical prison in London where many of the Elizabethan and Jamesian Puritans were imprisoned. "Clink" has since become a synonym for "prison" in England.

achievement, symbolized by the friendly way in which ministers of different denominations could foregather. Robert Jenney, one of the Anglican parsons, was joined by a Presbyterian minister in deploring the ravages wrought among their respective flocks by the Methodist preachers. A conversation of this sort was little likely to occur, for example in Scotland, where Anglican ministers were being persecuted by the Presbyterians, then in power.

This mutual forbearance was not incompatible with a good deal of name-calling. The harvest of souls in America was great, the reapers keenly competitive. The parsons, in particular, had little idea of what they would find when they came to the colonies, having left behind them an England where the Anglican church virtually controlled all spheres of national life. For them the sight of a Congregationalist justice, for example, must have been something of a shock. There was little in their previous reading that could have prepared them for the experience. History generally was almost ignored by the English universities, and American historical studies in Great Britain were only beginning with Robertson in Edinburgh. Otherwise the missionaries might have discovered, after a little reading, that the ideological impetus that had sent the first American colonists across three thousand miles of ocean had been provided by men who habitually spoke of the Church of England as the Second Beast in the Book of Revelations, and who used the word *bishop* to expel phlegm from the throat.

The first of the churches, other than Anglican ones, with which we are concerned, were or had been originally one with the Anglican sect. The national church, so strongly condemnatory of dissent, was about to proliferate two more "Nonconformist" churches. The description of "dissenting" would have been denied by both these groups, especially by the first of them, the Nonjurors. These gentlemen would have argued, with much politeness and a vast deal of learning that they *were* the Church of England, representing, as they did, the only churchmen who had remained faithful to the Anglican doctrines of the divine right of Kings, passive obedience, and nonresistance. The Nonjurors were the successors of those bishops and clergy who, at the accession of Dutch William in 1689, had refused to take the oaths of allegiance to the *de facto* sovereign, alleging that their previous oaths to William's predecessor, James II and VII, still bound them, that he was in fact still the lawful King, whatever Parliament might say. Such an attitude was not to be tolerated for an instant. Not recognize the Sovereign! They would be claiming the right to decide for themselves about matters of doctrine next. The Nonjurors were driven into the desert; that is, they lost their livings and employments, with little or no likelihood of ever getting any more. This virtually meant living in a desert, for, as Owen remarked, England might be the garden of the world, but very little grew there for nothing. The successors of these "nonswearers" or "nonjurors" refused to recognize Anne or the Hanoverians, whose officials thereupon subjected them to a persecution of varying degrees of severity, reaching a peak in Scotland. It is impossible not to like the Nonjurors; in them the Established Church of the eighteenth century had lost half its evil in losing all its grossness. Deprived by their own choice of the loaves and fishes that for so many Anglicans of the period seemed to comprise the whole of the church, they were able to cultivate at once a complete independence in matters of doctrine and a fine spirituality. Their tie with the Stuart Kings was a very tenuous one, and they must have represented in American eyes that "independent Church of England" which became the ideal of one American Anglican community, and which was afterwards to be realized in the

American Episcopalian Church. The chief difference between themselves and other Anglican parsons in the colonies lies in the fact that they were Jacobites, and would not, therefore, pray for King George. The colonies were, then, not such a strange place to find them as might be expected, for there were many Jacobites (lay "nonjurors" as it were) settled in them. One writer complained that a Jacobite was about to take up high office. "Colonel N . . .yth, nephew to the Earl of B . . .th, was lately very earnestly recommended by his Lordship to the rest of the proprietors of Carolina to be sent Chief Justice of that province, but is admitted to go only as secretary. [He is] so notorious a Jacobite as to have harboured Keys [who was afterwards hanged for being in the Assassination Plot]."[5] A letter from Henry Harris refers to Governor William Dummer, "who has on all occasions employed his authority and influence in protecting our excellent church and its ministers from open enemies and pretended friends, from Nonjurors and Jacobites. A defection from the present happy constitution and Protestant interest has of late much prevailed here in general. "Tis to be ascribed to Scotch Highlanders and other strangers who, flocking over into this country in great numbers, have fomented divisions and propagated their seditious principles among the inhabitants; but none did they so egregiously pervert as one John Checkley, who keeps a toyshop[6] in this place."[7] American vestries seem to have liked Nonjurors when they could get them, which is not surprising, as they were, as might be expected from the voluntary martyrdom they were undergoing, men of noble character,

---

5. 10/76. This is presumably the plot to kill William III as he drove home to Kensington Palace from his weekly hunting in Richmond Park and had to pass through a narrow and muddy lane between the Thames and Turnham Green. William told Parliament of the plot on February 24th, 1695.

6. Not a place where children's toys were sold, but a shop for snuff boxes, canes, quizzing glasses, and the like.

7. 6/? Letter from Henry Harris, June 22nd, 1724.

learned, discreet, and imbued with an overwhelming passion for religion. In this respect they often afforded a contrast with some of the other parsons. Very little has been heard of Nonjurors in America, with the exception of the famous John Talbot. This gentleman was one of the first three missionaries to land in America. Born in Wymondham in Norfolk, Talbot had been a Cambridge fellow before becoming rector of Fretherne in Gloucestershire in 1695. Not a Nonjuror in the ordinary sense of the word, since he had presumably taken the oath of allegiance to King William, he apparently had lingering doubts, for in 1702 he was in the unlikely kind of post of ship's chaplain, not the normal sort of position that a clergyman would have sought. The ship in which Talbot was chaplain was carrying George Keith and Patrick Gordon, the first two Society missionaries to the colonies. Talbot was so impressed with their mission that he decided to join them. He began a ministry in New Jersey, than which, says Bishop Perry "no labours have borne more enduring or more abundant fruit." It was said that he had been consecrated by the Nonjuring Bishops in England, in 1723 or 1724, and his salary was withdrawn. It was a significant step on the S.P.G.'s part; the harm that Talbot could do to the British government was infinitesimal. Nobody was likely to raise a rebellion for King James in the colonies, even though he had many friends there. It was the pride of the English bishops, who were determined that no one should assume their title, and the thoroughgoing Erastianism of the Society, terrified that George I might be offended, that led them to cast out one of the ablest missionaries in America, while still finding room for plenty of worthless fellows who were an offense to their congregations, and, goodness knows, no asset to their church, except that they were good Hanover men.

Mr. Talbot serves to recall John Urmston, a missionary

whom we have already met. Urmston was acting as curate for the incumbent of a Philadelphia church who was on sick leave in England. When the parson died, Urmston attempted to convert his temporary post into a permanent one; instead, the vestry chose "Mr. Talbot, the famous rector of Burlington in the Jersies." "He is a notorious Jacobite," Urmston told the Bishop, "and will not pray for the King and Royal Family by name; only says 'ye King and Prince,' by which 'tis obvious whom he means.[8] He hath often endeavoured to persuade me to do so too (little less than treason, I think, to go about to pervert the King's subjects from their duty and allegiance to his Majesty). He hath poisoned all the neighbouring clergy with his rebellious principles. They dare not pray otherwise than he does, when he is present. He caused many of my hearers to leave the Church. At last he gained his point, was accepted, and I kicked out very dirtily by the vestry, who pretended that the Bishop of London is not Diocesan, nor hath anything to do there more than another Bishop. So that any one that is lawfully ordained and licensed by any bishop (it matters not who, the Bishop of Rome I suppose albeit, and many more will say 'or any other') is capable of taking upon him any cure in America. I was not sorry for my removal from so precarious and slavish a place, where they require two sermons every Lord's Day, prayers all the week, and homilies on Festivals, besides abundance of funerals, christenings at home and sick to be visited. No settled salary [in] ye church."[9]

The grounds Talbot took up here are very interesting from the ecclesiastical point of view. Normally a parson in the colonies would have been either ordained by the Bishop of London, or would have his license; yet, as we shall see,

8. I.e., the exiled Stuarts at St. Germains: James and Prince James Edward Stuart.
9. John Urmston, Cecil County in Maryland, last of June 1724 Maryland Box.

there were parsons who arrived in America, having been ordained somewhere else, and began their ministry before they wrote, belatedly, to the Bishop for a licence. Again, why should a minister ordained by a Nonjuring Bishop not minister in America, when one American parson at least had been ordained by a Greek Orthodox Bishop, a prelate who could not be supposed to be a member of the Church of England at all? The suggestion that Talbot is ministering as a Nonjuring Bishop to the colonists seems to receive confirmation from this letter, as it also does from the following one. W. North told the Bishop that "the management of Christ Church in Philadelphia is in the hands of a vestry and two churchwardens, yearly elected and chosen by the people, and being they have all along claimed an independency [of] the Governor's authority, I am for peace sake obliged to be passive in things which are both indecent and disorderly, such as the suffering of some clergymen to read prayers and preach without mentioning the King, Prince, and Royal Family according to the rubric. So that myself and family, with such others as are of unquestioned loyalty to his present majesty, are deprived [of] the benefit of going to church least it may give encouragement to a spirit of disaffection. Should your Lordship therefore be pleased to cause some enquiry to be made in this matter, it would probably put an effectual stop to what in time may become more pernicious, for it is confidently reported here that some of these Nonjuring clergymen pretend to the authority and office of Bishops in the Church, which, however, they do not own, and I believe will not dare to practice, for I have publicly declared my resolution to prosecute with effect all those who either in doctrine or conversation shall attempt to debauch any of the people with schismatical and disloyal principles of that nature."[10]

10. 9/25. Philadelphia, July 20th, 1724. W. North.

Urmston was a particularly active persecutor of the Non-jurors in America, and Philip Stubbs, writing to the Bishop, "In obedience to your Lordship's commands just now laid upon me in the Cockpit," sent him two paragraphs of a letter of Urmston's relating to another Nonjuring clergy-man. The informer had moved from Philadelphia to Mary-land, and had by now presumably "fallen into disrepute."[11] His disreputable evidence was apparently enough to damn Dr. Welton, whom he describes in the following letter. "Dr. Welton makes a great noise amongst them [the Maryland-ers] by reason of his sufferings. He has brought with him to the value of three hundred pounds in guns and fishing tackle, with divers printed copies of his famous Altar Piece at Whitechapel. He has added a scrawl with words proceed-ing out of the mouth of the Bishop of Peterborough to this effect, as I am told—'I am not he that betrayed Christ, tho' as ready to do it as ever Judas was.'"[12] The British govern-ment, in response to these hints, ordered Welton's recall. Although perhaps unwilling to employ a person of known dishonest character, like Urmston, the Bishop encouraged him to act as a spy, and acted on the information he passed on. There was something very much amiss with a church whose colonial missions were being run as an espionage department for checking the loyalty to the home govern-ment of colonists. It does not seem unlikely that Urmston regained episcopal favor by his services in this respect, for he went on being employed in Maryland. It is pleasant to be able to record the end of his career as a parson informer. The Bishop's Commissary reported to him as follows: "The vestry of St. Stephens, Cecil County, was forming com-plaints against their rector, Mr. Urmston. Since which

11. Pascoe, p. 850.
12. 9/80. Westminster, April 16th, 1725. Philip Stubbs (Urmston's letter, dated Cecil County Maryland, 1724).

[time] they have complained of him, and I have heard them. He had been admonished before and since that had been often drunk on Sundays, when he should have performed divine service, and constantly on other days, and in his drunkeness guilty of many brutal actions. I have deprived him, but am apprehensive he will sue me for damages for the exercise of an authority for which there is no proper evidence."[13] Poor Mr. Henderson had less legal standing, in Maryland, than a commissary in a completely disestablished church, such as the Catholic Church in France in the nineteenth century, where at least a priest who had been condemned by the ecclesiastical courts could be prosecuted on the grounds that he was wearing a uniform to which he was not entitled. If Urmston, on the other hand, had stood his ground, it is difficult to see what Henderson could have done.

Urmston's deposition, however, did not help Welton, who was forced to fly the country. "Dr. Welton," wrote North, "having been duly served with his Majesty's writ of privy seal, commanding him upon his allegiance to return to Great Britain forthwith, in pursuance of which order the doctor did us the favour about four weeks ago to depart for Europe by the way of Lisbon."[14] "I understand Dr. Walton has left Philadelphia and is gone for Lisbon," said another observer. "He and the rest of the Nonjurors disagreed very [much] among themselves, in so much that they avoided one another's company. Mr. Talbot and Mr. Smith (who also differ very much in their sentiments of submission to our established government, have been with us in Maryland. They behaved themselves very modestly, avoided talking very much, and resolved to submit quietly to the

13. 3/177. Jacob Henderson, August 7th, 1731.
14. 9/61. W. North.

orders sent from England to prohibit their public officiating in any of the Churches, or to set up separate meetings."[15] It is worth noting that the Government was capable of acting promptly enough with regard to America when they thought their own safety menaced. They might delay a hundred and seventy-one years to arrange for a Bishop, but if there seemed to be a possibility of someone's undermining Hanoverian influence, that was a different matter. As a matter of fact, the Government played such a fine game, in this respect, that they cut their own throat. When sides were taken, in 1776, the Jacobites for the most part, ranged themselves on the British side, on the principle of "better the wrong King than none at all." It is, of course, of really prominent Jacobites that one thinks in this respect—people like Flora Mackdonald and Mackintosh of Mackintosh, but the many highlanders who became Tories should also be remembered. The Presbyterian Scots, who had supported the English government against Bonnie Prince Charlie and his father, were solidly revolutionary. Was it because the English were less supportable as allies than enemies?

Archibald Cumming told the Bishop: "I hope in a little time, by proper and moderate methods to cancel all the bad impressions the angry Doctor had given of his successor. Your Lordship will observe by his farewell sermon, printed here, in what a scurrilous manner he falls foul upon all the clergy of the present establishment. He is now in Lisbon, 'tis well if he be not got into a convent."[16] If Cumming hoped to extirpate Nonjuring churchmen completely he must have been disappointed, for there still continued to be instances here and there of parsons with Nonjuring sympathies, even

15. 21/66.
16. 9/25. Archibald Cumming, Philadelphia, October 19th, 1726.

if they did not express them very forcibly. "Mr. Ross," said Alexander Campbell, who was defending himself against a charge of immorality that had resulted in three other missionaries meeting in cabal, "trying" and condemning him, "Mr. Ross, one of Dr. Welton's accomplices, brother to my chief accuser, has the spirit and genius of an inquisitor. He is to this very day a Nonjuror."[17]

The true significance of Robert Welton and John Talbot is a revolutionary one; by administering confirmation to various Anglicans in the colonies they had anticipated history by fifty-nine years and created an independent American episcopate (unrecognized of course, except by those of Nonjuring sympathies), which approximated to that "independent Church of England" that was already the aim of some Anglicans in the colonies and that was to be realized after the Revolution. The Nonjurors refused to obey the King, even a Stuart King, if they felt that in so doing they were sacrificing the best interests of the church. They had not given up all in becoming free of the state in order to submit to mismanagement even from their lawful monarch; in that respect too, they were revolutionaries.[18]

Like the Nonjurors, the Methodists were revolutionaries, but in a different way. The missionaries, savage on the subject of Nonjurors, became virulent on the subject of Whitefield and his colleagues. They also wrote much more about them, and one of the justifications of this book is that it introduces some new material on the man who was perhaps the most prominent churchman of his time in the colonies. Many criticisms have been leveled against White-

17. 19/67. February 26th, 1727/8. Alexander Campbell, Apoquiniminek, February 26th, 1727. Campbell, as will be seen later, cleared himself on this occasion, but while at Brookhaven, New York, 1729-1732, was discharged (Pascoe, p. 855).
18. M. K. and C. Ritchie, "An Apology for the Aberdeen Evictions," *The Miscellany of the Third Spalding Club* Aberdeen, 1960).

field, but at least he was not lacking in missionary fervor. While waiting to go out to Georgia, he leaped into fame as a preacher in England, with people queueing up outside the church the night before. In spite of his popularity in England, and the material advantages that could be derived from it, he spent much of his life in the materially much less rewarding field of American missionary work.

American Anglicans were an almost ideal field for a religious revival. They had been ministered to for so long by men whose talent for religion was, to say the least, not conspicuous, that there is little surprising in the fact that Whitefield swept them up like chaff before the wind. His chief asset was his talent as a preacher. The normal Church of England sermon of the time was like a formal eighteenth-century pyrotechnical set piece. There was a good deal of cheerful light and not too much heat, with only the faintest whiff of sulphur. The congregation—one almost said the audience—knew what they had come to observe and were pleased with what they knew, so that they overlooked any slight spluttering amidst the flames of eloquence and the dim but carefully husbanded illumination of evidences. If, however—instead of taking off heavenwards and carrying its hearers gently with it—one of the rockets had left the stand vertically and fired off in the midst of the crowd, parting them amid anguished screams, illuminating every face with the flames of Hell, pointing at every heart with its burning finger, and scattering on them flakes like those of the perpetual fiery torment itself, that would be a Whitefieldian sermon. It is only fair to say that not everyone, even among the less sophisticated members of the congregation, was moved in this way. There is in the author's possession a copy of the 1738 edition of Dean Swift's works, on the flyleaf of which is scrawled a Whitefieldian anecdote by someone who was, no doubt, a witness to what occurred. The awakener was preaching to a congregation in Charleston (this would be in 1739, no doubt) and in the course of the sermon remarked: "Ah brother, this is a dismal bar to pass" (referring probably to the bar of judgment). A sailor in the church, however, taking this remark in the professional sense, replied "Damn your eyes, wait for a tide."

The general effect was, however, staggering. Parsons who had found the only physical response among their audience hitherto a nasal one, were enraged to see people burst into uncontrollable tears. Few had the courage to realize talents superior to their own, a grave omission, for it is only by the recognition of a higher competency amongst others that we can improve a technical skill. A few sensible churchmen were wholeheartedly admiring. Charles Blackwell, for instance, recognized the force behind the new phenomenon, and in a letter to the Bishop deplored the depredations likely to be made in the ranks of Anglican churchgoers when those other Methodist preachers, the Wesleys, came to America, as they seemed likely to do.[19] Missionary comment was pungent, and those of the parsons' congregations who had gone over were not spared. "The party set up by Whitefield here," said Robert Jenney, "hath affected the Presbyterians much more than the Church; not above two or three of character having left us, but the Presbyterians are almost broken to pieces. One of their preachers told me that he had scarce a dozen hearers when any of those 'vagrant preachers' (as he calls them) holds forth at Whitefields Building. There is also a great schism in Whitefield's congregation, occasioned by the German Count, who hath drawn off a great party from them. They hold distinct meetings, and are as warm against

19. 6/166. 1741.

one another as against other sects of religion. Whitefield's admirers give out that he will be here soon, which I give little credit to. But if he should come, God only knows what influence his presence may have upon a fickle, inconstant people, as the generality of the common sort here are."[20]

Alexander Howie used even stronger expressions. "Mr. Whitefield is arrived here, who by his indecent way of haranguing the populace seems to debase the dignity of religion, and by gathering together a dirty crowd in the dark night he acts the part of a Merry Andrew[21] in things sacred. He boasts of uncommon gifts. All our Quakers flock to hear him, and one of their preachers say[s] there never appeared so powerful a preacher since the days of George Fox."[22] Parson Gurton, in a letter to the Bishop, describes Whitefield as "A weak and wild visionary youth, whose head is filled with a jumble of *Antinominian* and Quaker notions, and turned with the populace everywhere running to hear him, owing wholly to his *talent for delivery* and not the doctrines he delivers."[23] The belief that Methodism was inseparable from the Wesleys and Whitefield died hard, and the parsons looked forward to the day when deprived of their support from the Church of England, they would disperse. "*Whitefield* will now trouble us no more nor are there now any of his followers in America that any of our clergy seem to have the least inclination of admitting to their pulpits."[24] It seems a poor epitaph, from a parson, for the man who, himself a Church of England minister, had awakened the Church from what seemed an immemorial sleep, but the judgment that the Methodists were in a tem-

20. 9/232. The Presbyterians were split into "Old Side" and "New Side" believers in 1745.
21. A buffoon.
22. ?/43. Oxford Pennsylvania, September 19th, 1739.
23. 10/74. A. Gurten's letter to the Bishop Charlestown, April 24th, 1740.
24. 9/42. Philadelphia, May 3rd, 1771.

porary decline was a true one. It is worth noting how the picture of religious life in the colonies is reinforced and illumined by the original letters of the parsons to London. The statement that the Quakers were attracted to White-field and his preaching, for instance, contradicts a state-ment by one of the ecclesiastical historians of the time that "the Friends were not friendly to a religion so different from theirs."[25]

The subject of the heresies entertained by the mis-sionaries, which might have been introduced earlier, has been delayed until this moment, because some of these unorthodox opinions, at least, were inspired by Methodist doctrine.

"One Mr. Stringer," wrote William Smith, "ordained by a *Greek Bishop* in England, now officiates at St. Pauls. I have never heard him but his preaching is said to be much in the *Whitefieldian* strain and very incoherent. Alas my Lord! The true manner of decorum of the Church seems too much departing from here, and to read the liturgy whatever else be added to it, or however little our canons, etc. be regarded is thought sufficient to denominate a man a churchman."[26] In keeping with the spirit of the time and profession in America, Stringer is being accused, on hearsay, by someone making a serious charge against him without bothering to verify whether it is a true one. Stringer was apparently rebuked for his deviation and allowed to continue in office, for a few years later we find him writing to the Bishop, thanking him for his forgiveness, presumably for this of-fense, in a letter that illustrates some of the characteristics of the Bishop's incoming mail at the time. "I am wholly at a loss for words to express the sentiments of gratitude which

25. Drummond, p. 117.
26. 7/63. William Smith, October 22nd, 1768.

predominate in my heart, when I reflect on my former irregularities and that your Lordship has not only forgiven me, but made me a minister of one of the best constituted churches in the world. Surely it is your Lordship's *glory to pass over a transgression*.' But what return shall I make your Lordship for such undeserved favours? If a cheerful submission to your Lordship's authority, a strict conformity to that church of which I have the honour to be a minister, a zealous and constant endeavour to promote harmony and virtue among the members of it, together with a behavior suitable to my character—if this is only what your Lordship expects of me, I hope I can assure you, that it is my fixed determination never to lose sight of such pleasing objects, but to pursue them to my latest breath."[27]

Mr. Peters, about whom more will be heard later, was another heretic, who was unfortunate enough to be reported verbatim by one of his colleagues. Shorthand notebooks seem to have been as much a feature of a clergyman's outfit in the colonies as gown and bands. He had held forth too strongly on the subject of natural religion (inherently evident principles of religion in nature as opposed to revelation). Affidavits were soon flying across the Atlantic to the effect that: "I Arthur Usher, missionary at Dover, in the Province of Pensilvania, do solemnly declare that I heard the Reverend Mr. Peters preach in Christs Church in Philadelphia on Whitsunday in ye present year 1737. In his discourse he seemed to extol and establish natural religion so far as to destroy the necessity of divine inspiration. The whole discourse seemed to be calculated to establish natural religion."[28] Ordinands waiting to make the risky trip to England for orders occasionally entertained heretical ideas

27. 9/46. William Stringer, Philadelphia, October 28th, 1773.
28. 9/79. Arthur Usher, September 18th, 1737.

as well; sometimes they were too honest to proceed further, feeling as they did, or to enter the cage with thirty-nine bars, at least until they had thought more deeply on the matter. One such was a Mr. Alison, who "hath entertained some scruple concerning the expressions of the Athanasian creed, which by his subscription he will be obliged to use in divine service, and he chooses to wait a while till he can get over them."[29]

One fundamental heresy, popular among a group of Anglican clergy and laymen in America, is of extreme importance, representing as it does an appreciation of the future development of the Church in America. It was this way of thinking that was—with a little help from General Washington and the French—to prevail. William Smith refers to it in a letter in which he discusses Mr. M'Clenachan's, or St. Paul's, Congregation in Philadelphia. "They," he writes, "are now neither numerous or of much note, but are still worthy to be brought into the bosom of our church if it can be done. Those among them who were true Churchmen have generally fallen off. The rest are a mixed sort, chiefly for an *independent Church of England*, a strange sort of church indeed! But the notion gains too much ground here, even among some of the clergy."[30] Strange or not, it has proved workable for a hundred and seventy-four years.

The Bishop was considered to be an authority on heresy even by people such as Baptist preachers. Here as elsewhere it is worth remembering the proverb that the greater will always attract the less. By virtue of its wealth, its authority, its long-seated tradition (in American terms), and such power as it had in the colonies, which was sometimes not

29. 9/62. June 27th, 1749.
30. 9/231. William Smith, Philadelphia, November 13th, 1766.

very great, the Church of England possessed in colonial times a powerful attraction for people of other denominations. Had that attraction been focused by the erection of a bishopric in America, it is possible that Anglicanism and at least some of the Nonconformist sects would have effected a compromise, such as subsisted in Restoration Scotland, where a Bishop presided over a synod of Presbyterian ministers.

"Though I am a poor man and of no figure in the world in comparison with your Lordship's," said Preacher Thomas, beginning significantly enough with a comparison between his worldly status and that of the master of Fulham Palace,

> yet being a man, a Christian, and sometimes a preacher of the Gospel, I do take the freedom, though with all due affection and reverence to your Lordship, in a matter of great importance, and wherein, if I can prevail on your Lordship to give your opinion I am persuaded it may do much good. The case in short is this. There is lately risen up a party in my neighbourhood of the Baptists' persuasion (of which communion I am also myself) who have advanced notions and opinions concerning the Son of God, and also the Holy Ghost, which are of a dangerous nature, as being not only, as I conceive, contrary to Scripture, the Analogy of Faith, the articles of other the reformed churches, but also the Primitive Church and Ancient Christian Councils, which if not by some effectual means suppressed I and others are afraid they will by degrees tend to much mischief in this country, and may, as a gangrene, spread to the disturbance of true religion in other adjacent places.
>
> William Thomas.
>
> I would only further mention (because) of my defect I borrowed the hand and pen of one Mr. Andrews Presbyterian minister in Philadelphia to draw up the above letter for me. He humbly sends his respect to your grace.[31]

---

31. Pennsylvania Box. Philadelphia in Pennsylvania, May 13th, 1743.

That a Baptist and a Presbyterian can now write to the Bishop of London asking for advice about backsliding Nonconformists indicates just how far along the path of tolerance America had come. It was not merely the Bishop's prestige that made him a respectable figure; he aggregated to himself the good qualities of the missionaries, among whom there was much good wool, in spite of a sprinkling of black sheep. Some of the parsons were well liked by everyone, whatever their convictions. "Honest Mr. Fraser," for instance, had "during the three years he has resided at Dover, done a great deal of good and gained the esteem and approbation of the people in general and even of different persuasions."[32] I have mentioned before the close relationship that existed between the Swedish Lutheran church and the Church of England, and that between the Anglicans and the Germans. They illustrate admirably how a large body can attract a small one. "It is not unknown." commented Richard Peters "to your Lordship that the Church of England in this province has been always in connection with the Swedish churches, and that the missionaries sent from Sweden, who have (except in a very few instances) been persons of eminent learning and piety, have at all times given us a very ready assistance, and done us many substantial services." The descendants of the Swedish colonists of Pennsylvania, the "old Swedish families" of whom the missionaries speak, were being ministered to, as we have seen already, by a parson at Oxford. Nor was there anything to stop a devout Anglican from going to the Swedish service in Philadelphia. When the governor had been quarreling with the incumbent of Christ Church, and felt that he could not sustain the royal dignity sufficiently under the eye of a malevolent, and possibly verbally critical

32. 9/92. Philadelphia, June 15th, 1776.

parson, he would step across the way to find what the pastor had to say that Sunday. A missionary commented on one such breach between the representatives of temporal and spiritual as follows: "Your Lordship's letters on Saturday last were delivered according to order to the Governor and Mr. Phillipps. They both promised obedience, but neither intends to perform. I waited on the Governor on Friday morning with Mr. Trent, the chief man in the church. So we went to the Churchwarden, and I demanded the church in your Lordship's name. So I went to church peaceably and quietly and brought the people back again, to the great joy of that city, but the Governor went away to the Swedish Church, which he understands as much as I do Arabic. I'm very glad to hear that R. Vesey is arrived safe at Boston, with the King's letter for his salary, for the Governor had put in such a Mayor as said he should never have it. He told me so himself. God help us for Government here *apud Americanos*,[33] I know not one of 'em good, especially the outlying parts."[34]

As has been said earlier, the arrival of a Bishop might have meant the fusion of the Anglican and some of the Lutheran and Calvinist churches, which were always on the point of close integration. "The congregation," (of Apoquiniminek), reported a missionary, "is very populous and consists not only of English but also many Dutch, as from Bohemia in Maryland, who are very desirous to hear the gospel preached in English."[35] How strong the desire for union was in some cases is shown by the following. "Petition of the representatives of the High German Church, called

33. I.e., among the Americans.
34. 9/74. Burlington, October 21st, 1715.
35. 9/88.

St. George's Church, in the city of Philadelphia." The petition:

> In all humble manner sheweth that your petitioners and other members of this congregation have at very great expense erected an handsome brick church in the said city for the service of Almighty God, being eighty two feet in length by fifty two feet in breadth. That your petitioners having felt the inconveniencies which have too often arisen in our churches, by being under the jurisdiction of a *coetus* here, or a foreign synod in Holland or Germany, are desirous of being under the protection of the Lord Bishop of London or whatever other Bishop our most gracious sovereign [should desire].[36]

If this is not a request for an American Bishop it is difficult to see what it is. Smaller Nonconformist churches, such as the Lutherans and Calvinists, saw in an American bishop a possible protector against the encroachments of the Congregationalists and Presbyterians. "The Quakers and [the] whole body of Germans declare loudly that we contend only for our natural rights, that we ought to have a Bishop, and they express their fear that if the Church has not a Bishop, and be enabled to grow as a balance to Presbyterians, the latter will so far get the upper hand as to endanger the religious liberties of all other Societies in America, if not in England."[37]

Although the Congregationalists were more numerous, the parsons seem to have seen in the Presbyterians their principal rivals. This may have been because the Presbyterians were a highly organized church, deriving some of their prestige from the mother country, with whose principal synod, that of Glasgow, the American Presbyterians

36. 9/87.
37. 9/63.

corresponded. They were, too, able to draw on the very large body of Presbyterian literature published in Great Britain, and to use it with effect in the colonies. Thus a book like Thomas Delaune's *A plea for the Nonconformists* could be referred to favorably by the author of a Scottish Presbyterian pamphlet and could also be welcomed in America and used in controversy. "There are some books of pernicious consequence to the interests of religion and the Church, industriously dispersed in this country, particularly the 'Rights of the Church,' De Launes, but especially 'The Independent Whig,' is extremely admired by all sorts of Dissenters and in a particular manner by the Quakers. And therefore answers to these vile pieces might be distributed among the people here with great advantage, especially the squires."[38] "There is nothing but writing in every newspaper," said William Smith. "The Church here is now very rudely treated by a malevolent set of writers, and though I could have wished our side had not given any cause, yet they must not be left unsupported, and I am determined now to contribute my mite, for great openings are given to detect their shameful misrepresentations."[39] Placed strategically as they were, with representatives in all the colonies, the Presbyterians must have seemed formidable to the parsons, especially since as it was from among their ranks that some of the most powerful "awakeners," such as Tennent, were to come.

The Anglicans made general complaints of "persecution" at the hands of their Nonconformist colleagues, complaints that, when analyzed, usually amounted to nothing more serious than Anglicans being hindered in their preaching, or Church of England men being forced to contribute to the

38. 2/113. James Honyman, Newport on Rhode Island, November 24th, 1725.
39. 9/46. William Smith, Philadelphia, May 6th, 1768.

support of a Congregationalist minister, or the like. "The sincere endeavours our honourable Governor has used," said a parson "(maugre all the attempts of interest and faction to sway and corrupt him) to prevent the ruin of the infant church at present unhappily divided by the artifice of John Moore and his adherents, will, I doubt not, only promise a general regard to him from the Society, but a large share by the assistance of your good offices in the esteem of that great and learned prelate, the Bishop of London. How highly necessary it is that (in a place thronged with all sorts of dissenters) so good a guard in time of persecution (notwithstanding any misrepresentations) should be confirmed under the crown when the government is surrendered. For we live in the midst of our enemies, who are glad of any handle to divide us and expose our conduct."[40]

Anglican ministers in the colonies had perhaps not entirely forgotten the circumstances of the year 1689, that of the "Glorious Revolution in New England." The unpopular Governor Andros had received the news of the intended landing of Dutch William while he was at Pemaquid, and had returned to Boston in March, taking refuge in the fort when the town rose in revolt. Cotton Mather, a very prominent preacher of the time, who had virtually adopted the Presbyterian platform, issued a manifesto defending the rebellion because of the danger from the French and Papists. Mather is interesting as representing almost the antithesis of archiepiscopal opinion, as can be seen from the excoriating comments in the margins of some of his sermons in Lambeth Palace, possibly issuing from a contemporary archiepiscopal fist. The anger of the populace seems in part to have been directed against the Church of England ministers, who had, of course, as Church of England men,

---

40. Philadelphia Box /15. Rev. Fra. Philipps, Philadelphia, May 22nd, 1715.

been supporters of King James. One parson at least believed it was the hope of the Presbyterians to exterminate their rivals. "Thus sir," he wrote, "you have a brief account of the detestable design, which was conceived in malice, nourished by falsehood and lies, and brought forth in tumult and rebellion, every way odious and detestable. Yet I must add how ugly soever it appears to the world, not half so horrid as some intended, and as it would most certainly have been had the least blood been split in the Revolution. For one of the preachers was for cutting the throats of all the established church. 'Then,' said he, very religiously, 'we shall never be troubled with them again.'" This attitude, if it existed, was an unfair one, since Andros had been on bad terms with the Bishop. Another contemporary letter, commenting on the injustice that the governor had displayed to the parsons, as well as to everyone else, remarked that the surest way of losing the governor's favor was to make an application for assistance to the Bishop's commissary.

A great source of dissension between Nonconformists and Anglicans was the taxing of Anglican citizens for a contribution to Nonconformist ministers. Daniel Mossom and other Anglican parson complained that their congregations were being assessed for contributions to the stipends of other ministers besides their own. "As to the church at Bristol," they remarked, "this, my Lord, is in as bad or rather a much worse condition than that at Marblehead. For they have committed to jail twenty persons who have refused to pay the rate made for the maintenance of the dissenting minister in that town and distrained upon the goods of the rest, an account of which we shall send to the Honourable Society, together with an humble petition to his majesty, imploring his protection."[41]

41. 2/114a.

Another bone of contention was the issue of marriage licenses by some Governors to Presbyterian ministers. These licenses, the parsons felt, should be issued only to themselves. The incumbent of Lewes sent in a petition against their issue to ministers of other denominations and added, "since Major Gordon's arrival here our present governor, he hath granted marriage licences promiscuously to be lodged with us and the Presbyterian ministers, a thing never done before in this government, except only in the last year of Sir William Keith, his immediate predecessor, when his fortune grew precarious, and he was willing by any means to raise money."[42]

Before leaving the Presbyterians, we may notice one of their ministers who attempted to become an Anglican parson. His apostasy is described in the following letter: "There is one Mr. Aiken that has officiated as a Presbyterian minister for some time but has been forced out of his congregation on account of some very bad conduct about his marriage, which was not only irregular but not performed till his wife was six or seven months gone with child. He declined answering before the Presbytery, called to examine this matter, and applied to us to recommend him to your Lordship. We resented his application as very insolent when he declined staying to clear himself with his own people. He then went to Maryland, and by showing some sort of certificate (which he got from part of his congregation in an artful way) he thereby procured the hands of some of our Church clergy in Maryland to recommend him. He is an artful man, and I thought it best to mention these circumstances."[43]

On the whole, the missionaries probably felt that they

42. Pennsylvania Box. William Becket, Lewes, Pennsylvania, March 15th, 1727.
43. 9/42. William Smith.

were fighting a losing battle against the forces of "dissent." The heroic Barton remarked that the county of Lancaster contained about forty thousand people, of whom only five hundred were Anglicans. The rest were "German Lutherans, Calvinists, Mennonists, Moravians, New Born, Dunkers, Presbyterians, Seceders, New Lights, Covenanters, Mountain-Men, Brownists, Independents, Papists, Quakers, Jews, etc. Amidst such a swarm of Sectaries, all indulg'd and favour'd by the Government, it is no wonder that the National Church should be borne down."[44] A weary tone comes into the ministers' letters as they describe their rivals' activities, as when the Maryland Clergy talk about "a sort of wandering pretenders to preaching, that came from New England and other places, which deluded not only the Protestant Dissenters from our church, but many of the churchmen themselves, by their extemporary prayers and preachments, for which they were admired by the people and got money of them."[45] Hugh Jones was equally in despair at the state of affairs in Maryland. "The great remissness and mean capacity of some, and the notorious immorality of others of my brethren here give great offence to many devout people, and occasion a contempt of the clergy amongst many of the laity, of which our Jesuits and the champions of dissension, enthusiasm, Deism and libertinism (with all which we abound) make no small advantage; especially seeing those sons of Eli are permitted to persevere with impunity and even without censure or admonition; since the cessation of the exercise of Mr. Henderson's Commissarial power. But these are evils, which you know (my Lord) require speedy remedies, even amongst the smallest numbers of people, but much more in this pop-

44. Pascoe, p. 36.
45. 3/145. May 14th, 17. Annapolis.

ulous infant province, consisting of upwards of thirty six thousand taxables who aren't a quarter of the whole number of souls."[46]

The church in America, as in England, suffered in its controversies with those of different religious persuasions by the excessive worldliness of some of its members. This aspect of colonial parsons (about which more will be said later) serves to introduce this survey of the last of the non-Anglican churches with which we are concerned, the Roman Catholic. Page, an intending missionary, had been turned back from his chosen parish. His story is then taken up by Smith in the following letter.

> Mr. Page never meant to settle among them but only to get into orders. Despairing ever to obtain recommendations from any of the clergy here, as his conduct had been very exceptionable the short time he was in America, he applied, just before he embarked, for letters, from Father Hardeing a worthy Jesuit in this town, to the Bishop of Canada, with a view to get ordained by him, and as he pretended, he meant afterwards to recant his errors and commence Preacher in our church. *Harding* who was always on good terms with us, discovering his duplicity and want of principle, refused to have anything to do with him. He then went among those people on our frontiers whom I have mentioned.[47]

Relations between priest and parson were not always so cordial as this. The missionaries saw in the Jesuits and other Roman clerics in America their most active, if not their most successful rivals. Hence the temptation, too often succumbed to by the Anglicans, of raising a party cry against the Catholics as emissaries of Rome and subverters of British liberties. This was an unfair charge to make, because

46. 3/47.
47. 9/229. Philadelphia, October 30th, 1773. William Smith.

although the Canadian clergy were one of the principal mainstays of resistance to the British, it was because they belonged to the French church (the most patriotic in Europe) rather than because they were Catholics. Had the Acadian priests been not Frenchmen, but, as the British government proposed, clerics from some other European country, they would not have presented the problem they did as a focus for resistance.

Many Roman Catholics had come to the colonies, some of them original founders, as in Maryland, others Irish and English immigrants who found in America the freedom to worship denied them at home. The incumbent of William and Mary parish, Maryland, noted that "the numbers of the families [is] unknown because there are so many Romans."[48] "My parish," said another missionary, "contains in it five hundred and fifty two families, of which many are Roman Catholics."[49] "Mr. Hall and Mr. Thomas Cockshutt," said an observer, "have most scandalously gone about the country here raising a faction against my Lord Baltimore, telling people he is a Roman Catholic, and they offerred to the clergy a petition to your Lordship to endeavour to have the government taken from him and given to the Governor, representing him and his guardian the Lord Guildford, to be Papists, and in short, has set the whole country in a ferment here with the danger from the Papists," whereas, the writer went on, they presented no problem, being quiet and peaceably behaved.[50]

Maryland Catholics were very diligent, as were their coreligionists in Pennsylvania. A missionary reported that "the Papists, who were quiet till now, begin to show their

48. 25/25.
49. 25/19.
50. 3/98.

heads, and by reason of the indulgence of the Charter granted by Mr. Penn to the inhabitants of this government, talk of building a Mass House here upon the borders of this county, where it joins the province of Maryland, where they have service performed by ye priest once in six weeks, and many from both governments flock to hear him."[51] The sheriff of Charles County, in accordance with an order of the Governor and Council, dated 16 August 1697, which commanded the local officers of the province to return lists of "what Romish priests and lay brothers are resident in their respective countrys and what churches, chapels and places of worship they have," reported that: "here are three Romish priests and one lay brother, viz. Richard Hubbert, friar, after the Order of St. Francis, William Hunter and Robert Brook, of the order of the Jesuits, William Burley, lay brother, and the places of worship are one chapel near Newport Town about forty foot long and about twenty foot wide."[52] "Through the late incumbent's long indisposition," remarked A.W. Holt, "the Papists reaped a very plentiful crop here, who are indefatigable, whose Priests are of the Jesuit order."[53]

Readers of Parkman will remember the challenges to disputes that used to be sent by the Roman Catholic clergy to their Protestant counterparts. Rainsford remarks that he has been constantly summoned to talks of this sort by the neighboring Jesuits.[54] For contests of this kind, the exhibition of a profound mental discipline, the products of the English universities were singularly unfitted. Even the normal educational skills were so severely neglected there that it is worth noting that the only Maryland missionary

51. 9/93.
52. 21/47.
53. ?/89.
54. 3/80.

who was unable to spell his own language properly, the incumbent of St. Michael's parish, Talbot County, was himself an Oxford don, who was sent abroad "To fulfill a condition on a fellowship founded by Sir Leolin Jenkins, in Jesus College, Oxon."[55]

Another viewpoint on metaphysical matters was represented by the "Deists," "infidels," or "libertines," people who did not subscribe to any religious belief—a fairly numerous number in the colonies, one would say, with Benjamin Franklin as their most important representative. A certain amount of the opposition to the Anglicans was put down to their account by the missionaries. Archibald Cumming saw in them the contrivers of a mob that had intended to rabble him. Here as elsewhere there is a suggestion that the "Deists," if not a political party themselves, were at least allied to one of the party cliques of the time. "By what I have said," remarks a minister,

> before the sermon enclosed, you will easily form a judgement of the great uneasiness Mr. Peters has created since his coming among us. I had at first formed a good opinion of the man, but since have good reason to think that he is very loose in his principles. He is much caressed by our modern infidels and concealed Deists, a mere tool to Andrew Hamilton, in whose measures your relation, Jeremy Langhorn is always engaged in. These, having the greatest share of influence in this place at present by their sly management and Peters by his intriguing talent getting into all companies, making one at all diversions, and by an affected action and gesture in the pulpit, have gained upon some men of sense and on many of the undiscerning crowd at the same time.[56]

It is very amusing in these letters to see someone who has

55. 25/15.
56. 9/148.

just been accused of something turning around and accusing someone else of the same thing. Here is an instance. "Of all his majestie's provinces," remarks the Jeremy Langhorne mentioned previously, "this province is the most mortifying place for Church of England ministers to be employed in. Infidelity and enthusiasm go hand in hand and are both jointly promoted (to our shame be it spoke) by some leading men here, whose power is employed upon all convenient occasions in brow beating the ministers of religion, ridiculing of things sacred and promoting such principles of libertinism as would startle a modest heathen."[57] Startling heathens seems to have been a favorite sport in colonial America (there were plenty of them about, in the person of the Indians), or at least a favorite expression, for some time later another correspondent wrote to the Bishop telling him, this time, that it was the parsons that would startle a sober heathen.[58]

A certain amount of the printed Anglican apologetics was directed at the atheists. "Your Lordship's letter upon the earthquake," said Parson Spencer, "I brought into this province, where it has been read by most people with the greatest approbation. I remember the Governor one day at his own table (where your Lordship's health has been several times drunk) observed that allowing the earthquake to be no threatening from the Almighty, yet, as your Lordship's letter tended to awaken the consciences of hardened sinners and to make mankind better, it certainly deserved the highest encomium."[59]

---

57. 9/181. Jeremy Langhorne, Oxford, Pennsylvania, August 19th, 1737.
58. Henry K. Rowe, *The History of Religion in the United States* (New York: Macmillan & Co., 1924), p. 14.
59. 3/204. Letter from A. Spencer.

4

Intellectual Life

*T*HOUGH the missionaries did not Anglicanize
America, their impact on the American culture was a
definitive one. It is perhaps their cultural activity that pro-
vides the best excuse for many of the other things they did.
Much may be forgiven to men who were in their small way
the exponents of the great age of British letters that was
unfolding on the other side of the Atlantic, who were at
least cursorily acquainted with the literature of the day, who
could write a correct and attractive style (as the reader will
probably agree by now) in a readable hand. The difference
between a culture fertilized by the infusion of English books
and schools and one that had more or less to struggle on as
best it could is seen in the difference between the letters
written by quite ordinary American colonists and those
written by Acadian merchants, people who were wealthy,
and therefore presumably able to afford the best educational facilities available.

One of the ways in which the missionaries added to the life of their communities was as the custodians of their parochial libraries. This was a feature of their work in which the Bishop was particularly interested, and a question in the series of demands for information that he made to the Maryland incumbents was "Have you a parochial library? If you have, are the books preserved and kept in good condition? Have you any particular rules and orders for the preserving of them? Are those rules and orders duly observed?"[1]

The Maryland missionaries could report only partially favorable progress. "Here is a tolerable good provincial library," remarked Samuel Skippon, the incumbent of St. Annes, Annapolis. "The books are well preserved."[2] "I have a small library," reported Parson Donaldson. "The books [are] kept by me in good condition, and according to Act of Assembly twice yearly visited by the vestry." Thomas Thomson, who obviously took a morose view of life, replied to the question in the words: "I have a parochial library, as well preserved and kept in as good condition as such things can well be expected to be kept."[3] The vicar of All Saints, Calvert county, sent in the information that there was "a small library in my possession, kept in good conditions, no rules, only subject to be visited by the vestry twice a year, by act of Assembly."[4] "There is a small parcel of good books sent there by Dr. Bray," remarks the rector of St. Michaels,[5] introducing the Andrew Carnegie of the time. Bray, who is just as active as a disseminator of books as a holder of visitations, was responsible for introducing many of the colonists to their first books, the only free books that many

1. 25/6.
2. *Ibid.*
3. 25/3. Thomas Thomson, Dorchester, Maryland.
4. 25/13. James Williamson, All Saints Parish, Calvert County.
5. 25/15.

of them could reach, and therefore in some cases the only books they ever read. No one except a few enthusiasts would feel very pleased at being turned loose amid a well-stocked Anglican library nowadays, but that is because the chief collecting period seems to have been between the Reformation and the eighteenth century. Collections made in Bishops' and Archbishops' libraries in the nineteenth century are usually contemptible enough, that at Lambeth being perhaps the worst. Bray's collections on the whole are very good ones, the types of books to be found among the free libraries that he gave to various Maryland parishes being illustrated by the following two catalogues of the period. The first is as follows:

> An Abridgement of ye Ecclesiastical laws,
> Three small books named "A Guide for Constables,"
> Six small books named "A familiar guide,"
> "The Poor Man's Help,"
> The catechism of ye church.

Bray's book gifts were not unlike the above list, though in fact this particular parcel did not emanate from him, as can be seen from the note below the list, which affirms that "These books were sent by Mr. Clare, Bookseller in St. Paul's Churchyard, by order of his grace the lord archbishop of Canterbury, etc. and received by.

Francis Nicholson."[6]

The second booklist is "A catalogue of the library of St. Paul's in Queen Anne's county.

> St. Cyprian,
> Lyndwood's "Provinciale,"
> Cameron's "Opera,"

---

6. Maryland Box /159. Maryland, port of Annapolis, February 15th, 1696/7.

G. Owerson's "Exposition of ye Church Catechism," two volumes,
Bishop Sanderson's "Sermons,"
Dr. Bray's "Bibliotheca Parochialis,"
Account of the Reformation of Mammon,
Dr. Comber's "Roman Forgeries,"
Dr. Comber's "Divine Right of Tithes,"
Kettlewell's "Measures of Man's Obedience,"
Kettlewell's "Practical Believer,"
Dr. Comber's "Ordination of Deacons, etc."
Dr. Lucas' "Enquiry After Happiness,"
Mr. Edward's "Sermons,"
Dr. Stillingfleet's "Ecclesiastical Cases,"
Dr. Goodmand's "Sermons,"
Bishop Kean's "Exposition of Ye Cathechism,"
"Defence of Ye Knowledge of Christ,"
Dugard's "Devine Law,"
Dr. Leighton's "Sermons,"
Spinck's "Trust in God,"
Aseticks,
Protestant Monastery,
Kettlewell's "Worthy Communicants,"
Baxter, "Poor Man's Family Book."[7]

The value of a library of this sort was manifold. It provided for the colonist the means of improving his reading and of knowing something about the setting forth of an argument and clothing it in an acceptable style. No one in his senses would sit down for an afternoon's amusement with a bound eighteenth-century collection of sermons, though if he did he might find out how much better preachers parsons were then than now, but it is not to be denied that the power of reasoning, of leading on the reader from point to point, from argument to argument, is much more strongly displayed in those collections than in, for example, some modern university theses. It was, in any

7. Maryland Box /32.

case, not amusement that the colonial reader sought when he took up a "good book" from the parochial library. Religious issues to him were real and living ones; he wished to improve his acquaintance with the tenets of his church, and in doing so he could feel, as a reader of the controversial literature it produced, a part of that wider Augustan world. Dr. Johnson in London might be reading just such a book and commenting on it to his friend Boswell. An interest in religion was necessary for a frontiersman. On the purely secular side, a reader of improving works would at least find himself introduced to concepts with which he was unfamiliar, but that were necessary for the complete education of a man. Anglican divines were still trying to prove the existence of God by Solar Activity, Natural Religion as revealed by the voyages of contemporary navigators, and the like.

What became of a library if someone did not make periodical gifts of books to it, and if it were not cared for, can be seen from a report where the incumbent states regretfully that "We have no proper library, but I have understood that there are a few books with this inscription on most of 'em 'that they belong to this parish and are to be lent,' scattered about in several hands. I have endeavoured to get 'em together, but have only got three of different sorts which I take care to preserve in as good condition as they were delivered me in."[8] There is something extremely attractive about this triadic library in Christ Church parish; no desperate and aimless wanderings along the shelves, wondering what to take out here. The minister's talk of "different sorts" of books, however, raises doubts as to his fitness for a librarian. "I have a small library in Durham parish," reported Mr. Maconchie. "All the books that I received when inducted are extant and kept in a good

8. 25/18. Christ Church parish on Kent Island in Maryland, June 3rd, 1724.

condition. The rules and orders for preserving them appointed by our General Assembly are complied with."[9] James Cox of Westminster parish mentions the existence of a Bray donation.[10] Often there is an impression that the incumbent, having got back all the parish books that had been out on loan, was taking good care not to let them out of his hands. One minister remarked, "There are twenty eight books (most of them small) belonging to the parish, and safe in my custody."[11] The usefulness of these parish books is perhaps best illustrated by the fact that there were so few books in private possession. Even Parson Rainsford, though he owned "a case with glass bottles in it, three drinking glasses, two dozen and a half of glass bottles, a quart mug [what does any temperate man want with a quart mug?], one punch bowl, one beer barrel, and two decanters," had in his possession no books.[12]

Even the books without which no Anglican service could legally be carried out were often wanting in America. Nathaniel Cotton told the Bishop that he wanted a Bible and a common prayer book, "as those formerly sent out by government [that is, the same as those which had been sent out before]. I have taken the liberty of mentioning to your Lordship our want of useful books."[13] Other incumbents such as Christopher Wilkinson mentioned their need of a Bible and prayer book.[14]

America was fortunate in that the period of missionary activity coincided with that of greatest activity in the Anglican schools in England, an activity that was carried over to

9. 25/24. Mr. Maconchie of Portobacco and Durham in Maryland.
10. 25/26. James Cox, Westminster parich.
11. 25/22.
12. 3/54.
13. Florida Box /83. Pensacola, Dec. 15th, 1768. Nathaniel Cotton.
14. July 29th, 1719. Christopher Wilkinson, Florida Box, /191.

the colonies. In part, the motive behind the founding of so many Anglican schools in England was a religious one; the Church was genuinely anxious that the many thousands of heathen children in England (many more than those in America, one would think) should know something about religion, and that the very successful efforts of the Nonconformists in providing schools and indeed very successful if unrecognized universities, should be combated. In part, too, at least later, it was felt that a little schooling might help to make the English poor more contented with their lot, and less likely to be led astray by the spokesmen of popular movements. Adam Smith had pointed out that the only way to avoid revolution was to educate the common people.

The colonial Americans did not have many opportunites of obtaining an education and were correspondingly modest in contrasting their attainments with those of people who had got their schooling in Britain. "We are now destitute of a minister," said the churchwardens of Pennsylvania parish "the gentleman not long since sent amongst us having thought fit to take a trip to the island of Barbadoes and there to accept of a parish, though we cannot learn that he had obtained leave either from your Lordship or of the Society, nor did he give us the least notice, all which we are willing to attribute to the want of a few more years, which, had he lived to have seen in the University, possibly might have added much to his understanding. We do not allege that he was not scholar enough for us, we ourselves having been so unhappy as to have but a slender education, but his indiscretion and rambling disposition gives great offence."[15] The vestry of St. Paul's parish stated that "many of the inhabitants of this place [are] ignorant illiterate people."[16] Sometimes this modesty seems a little unneces-

---

15. 9/143. October 29th, 1736, Province of Pennsylvania.
16. 21/133. Petition from the vestry of St. Paul's parish.

sary; there were many ignorant, illiterate people in England, too, but perhaps the colonists had forgotten this. George Ross remarks of his son, whom he was sending to England to get orders: "His learning, considering the manner of his education, which was private and at home, cannot bear the strictest examination, and therefore I hope your Lordship will be tender in this respect, considering whence he came and whither he is to return, he is very well instructed in the Greek and Latin tongues."[17]

Sometimes, for an American ordinand, a little additional "polish" at one of the home schools was considered suitable. "The bearer," wrote Jacob Henderson, the Bishop's commissary, in a letter of introduction, "is a young gentleman of this province, going to a school at Beverley in Yorkshire, desirous to confirmation. And therefore I thought fit to recommend him to your Lordship for that purpose and if your Lordship thinks fit to write to the Master of that school or to any other gentleman of the place in his favour, it would be taken by his mother as a particular obligation."[18]

Not many young American gentlemen could afford to have their education across the Atlantic. Most of them got it at home, and many of those from Anglican schoolmasters. Numbers of these masters, perhaps the greater part, had come out from Britain, and some of them were ordained. A vestry, writing to England in the hope of securing an incumbent, would hold out the office of schoolmaster as an added inducement to come to the parish; the vestry of Somerset County in Maryland hinted in their call to an English minister that he might have the public school, which was worth forty pounds a year.

The Bishop took great interest in so important a topic as schools, and one of the queries in his questionnaire read:

17. Fulham Papers, unassigned.
18. 21/69. Jacob Henderson, Maryland, August 19th, 1724.

"Have you in your parish any public school for the instruction of youth? If you have, is it endowed? And who is the master?"[19] In Maryland this produced various answers. Samuel Skippon, of St. Anne's, noted that there was a free school, with Michael Piper as the teacher.[20] In Great Choptauk parish there was "a public school endowed with twenty pounds Continental money, which is about fifteen pounds sterling yearly, for the which the master is obliged to teach ten charity scholars."[21] "Our government," noted another incumbent, more comprehensively, "has established a certain sum for erecting one [a school] in every county. There is about 250 lb in cash toward buying lands and building, and there will be about 20 lb per annum for a master, and we are in hopes [it] will improve into a greater sum every year, but things are in their infancy as yet."[22] British schoolmasters in the colonies were some of them talented men of exceptional character, others semiliterate and of no character at all. The latter seem somehow to predominate in the records. One of these, a Welshman, was described by an indignant compatriot as follows: "Meredith Jones has, by I know not what means imposed himself upon the Society and [has] been examined and approved by your Lordship, in order to be sent to the care of the school in Philadelphia. My Lord, he is a man who has shown a great want of honesty and good principles and therefore I am satisfied will not be thought a proper person to be intrusted with the education of youth. He ran away from this place after having run in debt as far as he could to many poor people of this place, and in one instance more criminal than common having gone off with some of the charity money given for the

19. 25/1.
20. 25/6.
21. 25/3.
22. 25/15. St. Michaels Parish, Talbot County, Maryland.

raising and support of a free school here."[23] Interesting
because he was a Louisbourg veteran, but apparently
equally rascally, was an Irishman called Cotgreve, or Cot-
grave, or Congreve. An acquaintance described him to the
Bishop as follows:

> It will be necessary then to give your Lordship a few anecdotes
> of the life of this man, so far as they have come to knowledge.
> He is a native of Ireland and hath been a good many years in
> America where by his own account he hath lived a vagrant life
> strolling from place to place through most of the colonies upon
> the Continent. He kept a house of public entertainment for
> some time at Philadelphia (of no good repute as I have reason
> to believe.) He was likewise in the army here, particularly at the
> siege of Louisbourg, where he belonged to the train of artil-
> lery. The war being over and strolling about as he had been
> accustomed to do, he came to Maryland and was appointed
> master of the Free School of the county of Prince George in
> which I live. There he married a wife who left him in a week's
> time, apprehending her life to be in danger from his violences.
> She had much reason, for he is an abandoned drunkard, and
> when drunk an outrageous madman. He remained with us
> about five or six months, and having got in debt left us abrupt-
> ly, in other words ran away, and I was in hopes I should have
> heard no more of him for ever. Your Lordship will judge what
> was my surprise and indignation upon receiving a letter from
> London, informing me that he was in holy orders.[24]

Nowadays one would think rather highly of someone
who had helped to haul the Yankee guns at Louisbourg,
and put irregularity of character down to the horrors of the
siege, but the fact that he had been a soldier was no recommendation for Cotgreve, just the reverse, in fact. Soldiers
were looked on as red-nosed, tippling idlers, useless loafers,

23. 3/64.
24. 3/64.

except in wartime of course, when public opinion underwent an abrupt change. "Our God and soldier we alike adore," said the proverb, "just in the time of danger, not before. The danger past and all our foes affrighted, God is forgotten and the soldier slighted." Another schoolmaster typical of the bad type, an American this time, was

One Chambers born in this city and educated a Presbyterian in New Jersey College, who had left Lancaster in this province on a charge of having a bastard, had gone into Maryland and got a title to a curacy with one Adams, with a certificate to your Lordship from some Maryland clergy, none of whom could have known him above a fortnight.

I have since received a letter from Mr. Barton with a deposition in the affair from one of the magistrates of Lancaster Borough, and find the story too true. The deposition is that of *Mary Kelleren,* before James Bickham, Esquire, dated 16 February 1768, who does depose and say, etc. "That the bastard wherewith she is pregnant was begotten upon her by Joseph Chambers, late of Lancaster, schoolmaster who is the father thereof and none else." On this deposition Chambers run off from Lancaster. Mr Barton in his letter of May 3rd. writes thus. "I am really sorry to hear Chambers has got off. The church will be ruined by such things. The girl is since delivered, and declared that Chambers and none else was the father of her child. This she did in the *pains and perils of child birth*. Chambers, after he went off, likewise wrote to Mr. Stout, whose servant the girl is, to provide her with lodging, necessaries, etc., "for all which he would pay," but had Mrs. Stout taken him at his word. She would have been left in the lurch for this, as well as he has done for his own board. Captain Singleton from Neward (where Chambers lived before) is here at present, and says "This is not the first crime of the sort in him." In short he is a person of no valuable qualifications, has read nothing, and can scarce write three lines correctly. His passions are violent and his conceit insufferable. He seems to prefer a life of dissipation to anything serious, and discovers a fondness for drink, gaming, and low company. If these charges require proofs they may be soon had. I beseech you send off *duplicates* and even *triplicates* of letters to the Bishop, else he will carry his point.[25]

Another hand now takes up the story of this schoolmaster. "Joseph Chambers is indeed a bad man. I am told he offered himself to your Lordship a certificate under the hand of a magistrate to clear himself of the guilt laid to his charge. This was a piece of artful villainy, for, if that certificate was not a forgery it was from a magistrate near forty miles from Lancaster, wherewith he was charged, tho' it was the first where there was issue and full proof made."[26]

Not all American teachers, of course, were like Chambers. The referees of Nathaniel Whitaker asserted that he "Hath for the space of fourteen months lived in the neighbourhood of this place, where he taught school, and behaved himself prudently, discreetly, and Christianly, and during the said time hath been a constant auditor and communicant in the Church of England,"[27] and we shall meet some admirable dominies later. The American school papers bring in many interesting people, among them Benjamin Franklin. His advice had been sought by an Anglican teacher, Sturgeon. Like some of the S.P.G. missionaries, Sturgeon had been doing good work arranging for the schooling of the Negro slaves. He describes the approaching visit of Franklin in the following unpublished letter.

Reverend Sir,
  I enclose to you a list of the school, and as Dr. Franklin is daily expected here his advice and assistance will enable me to put it on the best footing, of which I shall give you proper advice. I have drawn upon you for half a year's salary due to

25. 9/46. William Smith, Philadelphia, May 6th, 1768.
26. 7/63.
27. 21/203.

the mistress, which I make no doubt you will honour. Please to present my best regards to the monthly associates and assure them of my endeavours to instruct the negroes.[28]

Though the British were at war with some of the tribes at this time, the education of other Indian children was not forgotten. "The children under his care [that of Mr. Mashburn of Sarum], wrote Giles Rainsford, "are so well disciplined in the principles of our religion, and gave before me such an account of the grounds of it upon examination that strangely surprised me to hear 'em. He's seated between two Indian towns, and the Chowans would send to him their children for instruction, had they but money to pay for their schooling. And he promises, upon a small salary of twenty pound, yearly allowed him, to teach those children as well as our English that come to him gratis. I have represented to ye Society already and I hope your Lordship will use your interest with them for the encouragement of so pious a work. The country is mightily harassed by this Indian war, and truly the people are so much impoverished that I'm so far from expecting a support from them that I should rather beg the proprietors to forgive 'em their quit rents, the better to enable 'em to carry on the war. I like the country extremely well at present and hope the good I'm like to do in it will continue me much longer than I thought to have stayed. Though the Lords Proprietors have given two hundred pounds to the erecting of a church, yet the continuance of the war silences all advances to such an undertaking."[29]

Schoolteaching, never a well-paid profession, was par-

28. 9/215. July 1st, 1762. William Sturgeon, "To the Reverend Mr. John Waring at Mr. Bird's, Booksellers in Ave Mary Lane, near St. Pauls, London." Sturgeon, a Yale man, was missionary at Philadelphia 1747-1762.
29. 10/39. Giles Rainsford.

ticularly badly rewarded in North America at this time. William Keith comments on this, and on a particular schoolmaster's struggle with the difficulty of living on his salary, in the following letter.

I have likeways enclosed an estimate of the schoolmaster's profits which indeed I am ashamed of, but cannot help without some assistance from home, for which we must entirely rely upon your Lordship's and the Society's interposition. Mr. Skinner [the schoolmaster] himself is of a most prudent and unblameable conduct with everybody. He has not one enemy in the place, but many friends, nevertheless as matters now stand with him he cannot live by his employment, although he be justly esteemed with the few that are judges here to be the best grammarian and schoolmaster they ever knew in any part of America.[30]

Skinner describes his troubles in a letter that is very informative about the condition of American schools in general as well as his own, at this time:

Under your Lordship's protection, I have now taught school in Philadelphia two years and I plainly perceive that all the profits of the school, without the Royal Bounty restored, will not be found a tolerable subsistence. True it is, my Lord, I blame myself for having acted heedlessly in this affair, for had I adverted to the few hints your Lordship gave me of the place, I could not but expect to repent of such an undertaking. Your Lordship, considering my necessitous circumstances, may think my school is not numerous, but it is in a thriving condition. I have forty boys at present, four whereof are learning Greek, the rest Latin, for I have reduced it to a grammar school, that only being wanted in this place. I am obliged to give your Lordship some account of the inhabitants, whereof I may truly say three fourths are Quakers, having schoolmasters of their own persuasion, who teach Grammar as they can, and are

30. 9/219. Philadelphia. W. Keith, December 5th, 1720.

very much encouraged. And though the more understanding part of FRIENDS (if there is such a part among them) have trusted me with the education of their children, notwithstanding they are by far the richer, yet they are willing in their quarterly payments to copy after the poorer, and think they have laid me under no small obligation if they go the length of the church people, who are generally poor. And, what is more, having been educated in Wales, and the out parts of England (where half a crown quarterly is thought a large allowance) they scruple to give much more here, so that I have no set price, but am obliged to take what they think fit to give, which your Lordship may be well assured is little enough, so that I am straightened how to live and keep free of debt, though there is but little danger of the last, my credit being bad, and I have but small security of the first, for the Quakers are raising a fund for a schoolmaster of their own persuasion. Had I known the state of this country when I was with your Lordship, as well as now, I had applied to your Lorship for Holy Orders, of which, had your Lordship thought me worthy, I had been more useful both to myself and others. But the thoughts of a ragged gown and the bringing that Holy order into the least contempt by any unbecoming complaisance, to which poverty has reduced too many, seemed sufficient motives to dissuade me.[31]

So much for intellectual life in America, as illustrated in these letters. We shall not follow it into the sphere of higher education, and observe Timothy Cutler being hindered, in his researches into the foundation and origin of Harvard College, by the obstructive policy of the overseers there,[32] nor Governor Nicholson being flouted by the friends of Governor Andros because of his interest in "the college."[33] It is a regretful withdrawal, for the early days of the universities in America are among some of the most interesting things that the colonial period can show. Apart from re-

31. 9/223. Philadelphia, November 20th, 1720. William Skinner.
32. 6/43.
33. Francis Nicholson, Port of Annapolis, February 13th, 1696? Maryland Box. 143.

turning to look at the first Master of Arts certificate ever issued by Columbia University, we shall stand aside from these first steps of the intellectual giants, first steps that, unpromising as some of them were, had still attracted the attention of European wits to the extent that, when war broke out, there were not wanting those who would foretell how "Philadelphia will become the Oxford of the New World, and the town of Cambridge, in America, will cause that of Cambridge, in England, to be forgotten."[34]

34. "Philadelphie sera l'Oxford de l'Amerique; et l'Université de Cambridge dans la Nouvelle Angleterre fera oublier qu'il y en a eu une autre du même nom dans la Grande Bretagne" (Journal de Genève [10 July 1779]). These prophetic words seem to deserve a little reportage. The *Journal Historique et Politique de Genève*, a French-language journal, was, in spite of its name, not published at Geneva. (I am indebted to Miss M. F. Chevalier, of the Henry E. Huntingdon Library for this information.) Possibly it gave itself this title in the hope that French readers might buy it under the misapprehension that it contained more news than the censored French papers. It seems possible that the *Journal* had an American war correspondent; it certainly published a good deal of news from the Revolution. It never seems to be quoted in accounts of the war however, and this neglect is no doubt due to the scarcity of sets. There is, for example, no set in the Huntingdon Library, and my own very incomplete bound volume of it was the fruit of long searching along the Seine bookstalls.

5

"Our Rascally Clergy"

*T*HE American Church inherited its vices, as well as its virtues, from the Anglican Church in England. While it was usually a strong cultural force, in touch with many of the most advanced ideas of the time—the education of Negro children and the amelioration of slave conditions being among them, it was, also, in some of its members, very worldly. "Did your Lordship correspond with some laymen in this province," wrote one of them, named Jonathan Hughes, "you would be better able to judge of things than by getting all your information from the clergy only. I do not mean by this to represent all the clergy here as dishonest men, nor shall I admit that they are all honest neither, but I shall divide them into three classes. First those that I well know and believe to be Christians, secondly those that I also know but have good cause to suspect their sincerity, and thirdly, those that I do not know, and therefore shall say nothing of them."[1]

The reader will have to follow Hughes's example, and divide the parsons into good ones, bad ones, and those about whom it is impossible to form an opinion. On the whole the official records are a hindrance, rather than a help, in doing this. Clergymen's opinions on others of their cloth are rarely satisfactory to the historian. They may tend to support a parson, because of fellow feeling, or condemn him, from the opposite kind of feeling, professional jealousy. This tendency can be seen most strongly in the parsons' condemnation of those of their church who were Methodists. If the Bishop was to believe everything that the parsons said about each other, he would have before him a black picture indeed, for they rarely missed an opportunity to backbite one another. This tendency is illustrated by a letter from a Maryland parson. "The ships are all sailed out of our river, this one only excepted, and she lies so low down that I was obliged to ride forty mile to send this by her. I writ two letters by two several ships and in them mentioned something of the scandalous behaviour of some of our rascally clergy. Mr. Williamson is grown notorious and con-summate in villainy. He is really an original for drinking and swearing. Mr. Donaldson is so vile that the other day, being sent for to a dying person, came drunk, and the poor expiring soul, seeing his hopeful parson in that condition, refused the Sacrament at his hands and died without it. Mr. Maconchie is a mere nuisance, and makes ye church stink. He fights, and drinks on all occasions, and as I am told *alienas permolet uxores*.[2] You must think, sir I take no plea-sure in raking into the filth of the clergy's lives. If there were but a bare probability of these mens' leaving their idle courses, but since there remains no hopes of it, I think a

1. 9/72. February 19, 1765. Jonathan Hughes.
2. Forces his attentions on the wives of others.

check would be very seasonable without discovering the informer."[3]

Rainsford was, as has been seen, an unexceptionable clergyman in some ways, a good example of that kind of frontier parson whom the age brought out in numbers, and who went on with his duty, undeterred by the worst the Indians and the French could do. Here, however, he is being less than a man, certainly less then a clergyman, in sending a denunciation, which he wishes to remain anonymous, about two of his fellow clergymen. The proper persons to compain of an incumbent's conduct to his bishop are his churchwardens. If those of the two reverend gentlemen mentioned above were content not to do so, what business was it of Rainsford's? If, on the other hand, they had denounced him, there was no need for the interference of a third person. It was hardly worth while riding forty miles to accuse someone anonymously on hearsay, but it was a thing that was often done in America at this time. One views the American parsons through a sort of miasmic vapor of report—good report by their friends, and ill by their enemies. What is one to believe? Is it possible to form a conclusion about what these people were really like? Hardly. What was more to the question, it was impossible for the Bishop, three thousand miles away, to do so, as one of his advisers ruefully reminded him. Yet he was supposed to be responsible for them. Theoretically it should be possible to come to a precise conclusion, at least about the S.P.G. missionaries, because their careers have, for the most part, been recorded in the official papers in London. Thus we find that, according to the official Society history, there were three hundred and nine missionaries, of whom thirteen were dismissed for neglect of duty or other unsatisfac-

3. Maryland Box II, Patuxen River, Maryland, August 10th, 1724. Giles Rainsford.

tory conduct, during the period 1702-1785. This gives an average of about one in twenty-three ministers dismissed for misconduct, on the face of it a very good record, considering what contemporary England was like. It must be remembered, however, that it was not the regular procedure to give a suspected missionary a regular trial, as would be necessary in England, and consequently it is possible to suspect the validity of these demissions. If a man is not to be given a fair trial, it is possible to suggest that he may have done almost anything, and get rid of him. This seems to have been the case with Talbot, for example. It will be remembered that there was never any proof that he was a Nonjuring bishop; he was merely suspected to have been one.[4] Again there is this element of secret vote in the case of Alexander Campbell, which is mentioned below, in which three of his fellow ministers met and "condemned" him.

On paper the regulations of the Society were so rigid that it should have been impossible for a black sheep to slip between them. Archdeacons and Bishops were invited to recommend candidates, having regard to their age, condition of life, whether married or single, temper, prudence, learning, sober and pious conversation, zeal for the Christian religion and diligence in his holy calling, affection for the present government, and his conformity to the doctrine and discipline of the Church of England. The desirable qualities were listed in that order, with an affirmation of loyalty to King George coming before conformity to Anglicanism.

From the time missionaries received their appointment, during the rest of their stay in London, and in fact up to the end of their official lives in the colonies, their conduct was regulated by a minute code of thirty-seven articles. These

4. The Missionary Roll. Pascoe, p. 849, has provided these statistics.

dealt with almost everything that could concern a minister. When living in London, he was to lodge, "not in any public house, but at some bookseller's or in other private and reputable families."[5] This raises the problem of why booksellers should be pitched on as being more respectable than other people. In view of the reputation given them by the authors who worked for them, one would have supposed just the contrary, but it is worth mentioning that there was in London during the colonial period one very honest bookseller, who always returned to the Archbishop's library books that had the Archiepiscopal stamp in them, and that he had bought in error, even though he had paid good money for them to the (clerical?) readers who had sold them to him. On the other hand, some booksellers, such as Isaac Bickerstaff, if we can believe Dean Swift, made most of their money by publishing immoral books. Some of the other injunctions to ministers seem to have been more honored in the breach than the observance. In particular they did not "endeavour to preserve a Christian Agreement and Union one with another,"[6] being, for the most part, most noticeably hostile to one another. They did not, except in a few cases, get near enough to the "heathen" to conduct very vigorous missionary activity among them, so the instructions from the Society as to how they were to proceed, "in their instructing heathens and infidels, with the principles of natural religion, appealing to their reason and conscience, and thence proceed to shew them the necessity of Revelation,"[7] were for the most part wasted.

Those "bad" characters whom the Society dismissed are marked in their official history with the Greek character ϕ,

5. Pascoe, p.837.
6. *Ibid.*, p.838
7. Pascoe, pp. 836 The statistics that follow are from Pascoe's figures, p. 849, but it must be remembered that he did not give all the information about all the missionaries, but it is possible to fill out the "Missionary Roll" from Pascoe's book in some instances.

whether because this makes the same sound as the English "fie," in "fie for shame!" or because, like James Boswell, they used it to stand for the Greek word φιλια meaning "love" is not said. The duration of tenure of the thirteen dismissed missionaries is worth noting. The time that they served was, on the average, ten years. Thus they could have lived ten years in their parish without being considered bad enough to be got rid of. Now, of the three hundred and thirty-five missionaries serving in what is now the United States during the colonial period, there were one hundred and sixty-eight who served for five years or less. The number of those serving for one year was sixty-two, that is, over a third of those who served for five years and under and almost one-sixth of the whole. About half of those either resigned or died in the first year. About a quarter died, about a quarter resigned, about a quarter were transferred, and the fate of the rest is unknown. Probably those who were transferred requested it themselves. The resignations cover eight φ, and one who simply "left," one who was recalled (to England?), and one who is recorded as having "dismissed himself." It does not then seem impossible that there could have been a good many bad characters among those who resigned, seeing that it took, on the average, five years to get rid of the very bad ones. Possibly some of the ones who resigned were "advised" to do so. In fairness to American congregations it must be said that they did not, on the whole, write many letters of complaint about their parsons to the Bishop. They might tell the parson to his face that he talked nonsense, or that he only went to preach at Elk Ridge because there was a pretty face in the congregation, but usually, except in a really scandalous case of drunkenness, for example, they were content not to pass this criticism on to the Bishop. This moderation was not imitated by the clergy. When the Bishop read his post bag from America, he could be reasonably certain a large part

of it would consist of violent denunciations of clergy by
clergy, sometimes two parsons accusing each other of the
same offense. The writers would have been hard put to it to
sustain some of the charges that they made against their
colleagues, and in particular instances it is sometimes possible to prove they were baseless. When Urmston accuses
Rainsford of having returned to England after having
preached once, we know the accusation to be false. Why
then were these charges made? In some cases it is possible
that by blackening a colleague's character, a parson might
hope to succeed to his congregation and living, and there
there may be a material motive. This cannot always have
been the case however; the American colonies were the
world's largest diocese; new settlements were continually
being carved out by the Americans' axes. There were never
enough clergymen to go around. Why then should the
clergy be at such pains to send home bad reports of one
another? It is difficult to escape the conclusion that the
Bishop, perhaps in his private conversation with each missionary before he went overseas, encouraged them to do so.
Compared with the English clergy, the American parsons
were not noticeably immoral. In a country where a Durham
incumbent, visiting Yorkshire, could remark casually in his
diary that the Yorkshire clergy were every way as debauched as those whom he knew at home, and where one of
the York prebends (Lawrence Sterne) spent the last year or
so of his life arranging the prebendal house to accommo-
date a married lady, whom he was trying to entice away
from her husband, while he was dying of a disease con-
tracted from another woman, it was hardly likely that the
morals of the American clergy (many of whom, it must be
remembered, had left their wives at home, or who could
not, if their stipend was poor, or if the Society had not paid
them for three years, afford to marry) would attract much

attention. What is to be reprobated is the fact that the
Society obviously put loyalty to the King before other
characteristics in a parson. Men like Edward Bass of New-
bury, John Talbot, and Samuel Fayerweather of Naragan-
sett were dismissed by the Society, not because they got
drunk, or took other men's wives, but because they were
thought not enthusiastic enough supporters of King
George. On the other hand, people like our old friend
Cosgreve, formerly of the Artillery, who had his character
given a few pages back, became ministers apparently without difficulty, and continued in that office.[8]

When it is stated that the American parsons were, to say
the least, no worse than English ones, it must still be borne
in mind that if anyone had a particularly strong reason for
getting out of England quickly , his mind seemed to turn (if
he were in orders) toward the American church. In consequence of this, the lives of some of the clergy who came
out to the colonies are much more interesting than could
have been hoped. Particularly *romantick* is the story of Mr.
Peters, described for us shortly in the following letter to the
Bishop from his relative, Jeremy Langhorne. Langhorne
suggests that he is a suitable candidate for an assistantship
in Philadelphia in these words. "By his abilities and conduct
he is capable of giving your church a reputation which it has
wanted in these parts by a bad ministry. He is a Lancashire
man, the son of Mr. Ralph Peters, town clerk of Liverpool,
who for the sake of a good education sent him very young to
Westminster School, which he went through before he was
fifteen, and he had particular favors shown him by Doctor
Friend. Here it was that he was deluded by a servant maid

8. Pascoe, p. 850. His identity with the Cosgreve described earlier is established by
the entry "A Carolina Schoolmaster, whose return passage on his ordination in
1765 was aided by the Society."

where he lodged into a Fleet[9] marriage.[10] His parents hearing of it, altered their mind as to the remaining part of his education and instead of sending him to Oxford, removed him to Leyden, where he was three years. Upon his return he was put to study the law under the care of Mr. Bootle of the Inner Temple by the command of his father, against his will, for he was always inclined to go into orders. He was five years in the Inner Temple, and although capable of practicing the law to great advantage, yet his religious turn of mind increasing, his father was prevailed upon to let him take orders. While young Peters was the incumbent of Latham Chapel, to which his old tutor in the law, Mr. Bootle, had been complaisant enough to present him. Cupid appeared, crowned in strawberry leaves, and he fell in love with the Earl of Derby's daughter. Peters "was there taken notice of by the late Earl of Derby and entrusted with the education of two of his relations, and lived with his Lordship in his palace of Knowsley, till the first of July last. During all this time knowing in what a base manner he was tricked by the woman, he never cohabited with her, nor gave himself any trouble about her, and about three years ago, upon his return from Leyden, where he had been to place the two young gentlemen, my Lord's relations, he was congratulated by all his friends in a public manner for his deliverance from the woman, who, they told him, had died while he was in Holland and her death came confirmed afterwards by several letters from his friends in London. Taking himself to be at full liberty, he made his public addresses to Miss Stanley, sister to the young gentlemen whom he had placed at Leyden and married her, Christmas twelve months.

9. A marriage performed by a parson in the Fleet Prison, legal, but not requiring banns.
10. A sort of London equivalent of Gretna Green.

"In June last it was discovered that the woman was alive, upon which he voluntarily, with the consent of his wife, came over here."[11] Which wife, one wants to ask? It is, however, quite obvious who is meant, and it is equally obvious that Peters was not quite so blameless as his friends make him out to be. There were such things as burial entries, even in those days, and he could, had he wanted to, have secured proof of his wife's death. At the same time it is difficult not to feel sorry for Peters; he certainly seems to have been trapped into his first marriage, and remarriage to a Miss Stanley must have seemed very tempting to a young man of the eighteenth century, whatever the girl was like. The obvious course to take, divorce, was difficult, because although the Anglican Church as we know it had come into being because someone wanted a divorce, and its second founder, Laud, had owed his rise to power in part to his timely remarriage of a divorced person, divorces were nevertheless distributed with a very sparing hand. Even a divorce could not help Peters now, however; he had committed bigamy, a very serious offense in those days, a felony, in fact, and he was liable to instant arrest. The North American colonies had been founded by people who wanted to put three thousand miles of ocean between themselves and the English legal authorities, and they still continued their beneficent function. To the colonies Peters went, much to the disapproval of his more conventional colleagues, though he was not the only bigamist parson in America by any means. A few years before, James Honyman had described to the Bishop the harm done by the presence "in that promising nursery" of Providence, Rhode Island, of a twice-married minister.[12]

11. 9/58. May 28, 1736. Jeremy Langhorne.
12. 6/104. December 9th, 1728, Providence Rhode Island. James Honyman.

The Non-Anglicans did not fail to make capital out of Peter's felony. "Some among the sectaries, "wrote a minister," reproach us for having entertained one as our teacher who (as they say) was forced to fly from justice. T'was near half a year after his arrival here before I knew any thing of his having two wives. The reason of his leaving England I and many others were told (not indeed by himself) was his having married an heiress, and that he must keep out of the way, till her friends were mollified."[13] It was true in a way, of course. "Friends" in eighteenth-century parlance meant "family," and the Duke was hardly likely to be pleased at having a prospective convict for a relative.

Once arrived at his cure, Peters seems to have performed his duties punctually; the incumbent for whom he was acting as curate testified that "Mr. Richard Peters, a clergyman, arrived here from England, has assisted in our church and for the last five weeks has himself gone through the whole duty; for during that time I have been under the surgeon's hands, and have suffered much by incisions of caustic for ye cure of a fistula; but am now, thank God, in a fair way of recovery."[14] In spite of this, however, the man's past record told against him and he had to abandon the exercise of his office. "Such discouragement," as he put it, "as I have received, and so much ill treatment from persons at whose hands I deserved much better made me determine to suspend the exercise of my function. In the meantime the Honourable the Proprietor of this province, seeing me quite at leisure and knowing my education had been at the Temple was pleased to make me an offer of the place of Secretary of the Land Office for this province and the three lower counties, an honourable and beneficial office."[15] Ev-

13. 9/148. Archibald Cummings, July 22nd, 1737.
14. 9/24. Philadelphia, May 11th, 1735.
15. 9/190. Richard Peters, Philadelphia, November 29th, 1737.

erything about a parson could be viewed in two different lights—as the world saw it, and in the light in which his reverend colleagues were pleased to represent it. Thus, while the fact that Peters's having been at the Temple, the great school of young English lawyers, where they dined in hall, listened to the arguments of the barristers, issued after them to the courts, and studied in their chambers, was a recommendation to the proprietors, in the eyes of his fellow parsons it was a disadvantage. "To give you an instance of Mr. Peter's caballing and intriguing with our vestry," wrote a parson, "and his talent at underhand management, which no doubt he learnt being bred an underling to the law, I send a copy of what he wrote to ye pretended vestry."[16]

In Peters's case, constant letter-writing by his colleagues seems to have made a bad situation worse. If they had kept quiet about his bad luck in England everything might have passed off without scandal. Silence on the part of a fellow cleric's shortcomings was the very last thing to be found in a colonial parson, however, as the next few pages will show. It could honestly be said, however, that no amount of talking was likely to worsen the case of some parsons, who were so bad that there was nothing good to be said about them at all. The vestry of St. Paul's parish, Baltimore, petitioned against their incumbent as follows: "Many of the inhabitants of this place, being ignorant, illiterate people, not knowing good from evil, and leading a riotous course of life, profaning the Lord's Day with drunkeness and many other sorts of vice, the reason of most, if not all these irregularities, we verily believe in our conscience, proceed from the bad example of our minister, he being a very weak man, not knowing how to admonish, nor dare not tell them of the mote that is in their eyes, for fear they should bid him

16. 9/184. Undated.

to pluck the beam out of his own."[17] Mr. Tibbs, St. Paul's incumbent, was arraigned under the following heads. "First. That he is a common drunkard. Second. That he is guilty of such actions in his drink that will make a modest man blush to name them. Third. That he refuses to go to private houses to baptize children that are sick, and not able to be brought to the church without being paid for it. Fourthly. That he will be drunk on his taking the Sacrament before it can be supposed that the Bread and Wine is digested in his stomach."[18]

We need not imitate the S.P.G. missionaries and condemn someone unheard. Mr. Tibbs had a defense, and on the face of it a reasonable one—a defense often put forward before and since—namely, that the parishioners, having taken a dislike to him, could find nothing good to say about him. "I was accused," he says, "for not keeping my stops [in conducting the service?], preaching of nonsense, 'Sorry Fellow,' and how he could teach me, and ye like. Second. He accused me of cheating ye parish of five thousand pound of tobacco. When a certain young woman was married on Elk Ridge I left off preaching there,' or thus 'I went more for the sake of the young woman than to preach ye Gospel.' Thirdly. How I came more for the fleece than the flock and ye like. Fourthly. He thought it strange why the people should pay more for marriages now than they did formerly."[19]

It goes without saying that the poor Bishop, three thousand miles away, was quite incapable of distinguishing between the sheep and the goats. It was a position to which the government of his transmarine diocese had quite accus-

17. 21/33. "Petition from the Vestry of St. Paul's parish in the county of Baltimore."
18. *Ibid.*
19. 21/133.

tomed him, as an official of his remarked in the following letter.

"I am utterly at a loss to think how your Lordship will be able to determine in this affair with safety and honour. I am inclined to fear, from the experience I had of the West India controversies that there may be some truth, and a great deal of resentment on both sides. The distance is great, the persons that write, are strangers to your Lordship. Personal piques will happen to arise and will grow and swell into public prosecutions."[20] A crop of libel suits usually followed any attempt at "correction," the censuring of clergymen for offenses against morality. Alexander Campbell, as we will see, was "tried" by three of his fellow clergy, for immorality, and proceeded against them afterwards in a civil court. The policing of the morals of the clergy was hardly helped by the occasional commissaries that the Bishop sent out, for their position was an insecure one. How, indeed could they be recognized as commissaries of a bishop, when there was no bishop resident in America? In many instances their power came to depend on the degree of favor with which they were regarded by the Governor and Assembly. "I have deprived him," wrote a commissary about a drunken parson, "but am apprehensive he will sue me for damages for the exercise of an authority for which there is no proper evidence."[21] Commissaries in America tended to fall between two stools. The lay stool was that ordinary parishioners regarded them as champions of the rights of the church, which indeed they were, people who had come out to the colonies to make the colonists pay their church dues. Hence they were knocked about by anticlerical Americans. The clerical stool consisted in the fact that the parsons regarded the commissaries as the home

20. ?/4 Parsongreen (England), August 11th, 1715. W. Hall.
21. 3/177. Jacob Henderson, August 7th, 1731.

government's apology for a Bishop, quite correctly of course. They thought of them as a half-hearted attempt to provide for their needs that ought not to be encouraged, in the hope that if the commissary scheme fell through, people at home might finally decide to create an American bishop. Hence commissaries were not popular with anyone. "They are really good people," said a Philadelphia parson, referring to the clergy of his native town in a rather patronizing fashion, "And some of them [are] very sensible, as Dr. Chandler, Mr. Seabury, Mr. M'Kean, and Mr. Cook. In short they are all diligent in their cures, and have religion at heart, but for all this they cannot observe any temper in the affair of Bishops, and it is just so with the New York clergy, as I hear, and indeed have seen a little of it in some of them. They have got it into their head that the appointment of Commissaries is like throwing cold water on the design of sending us Bishops and will oppose all commissional powers with all their might."[22] The commissary's was no easy task. "This day," wrote a missionary, "we have it in our public American Gazette that what I, with many other of the ministers of the Church of England earnestly wished for is at length obtained. But my Lord, pardon my boldness, the utmost care is to be taken in appointing your Lordship's commissaries. Men of cool heads and unbiassed judgements, whose charity is at least equal to their zeal, and yet whose zeal is not quite extinguished by their charity."[23] The writer of that letter was Alexander Campbell, and his case illustrates the need for a Bishop with the ordinary powers of ecclesiastical judgment in America. Campbell had been accused and "judged" by three of his fellow missionaries on a charge of immorality. Being a Scot, as many of the mis-

22. 9/32.
23. 9/69. Alexander Campbell, Newcastle upon De la War, July 8th, 1728.

sionaries were, he had a good knowledge of both civil and canon law, on which Scots law was based, and which was also used in the ecclesiastical courts, as against English Common Law, the old feudal law, which was used in civil courts. He was therefore able to put a fairly good case for himself to the Bishop. The fact that he sued one of his opponents for slander in a civil court and won his case suggests that the charges brought against him were flimsy ones. Nevertheless he was dismissed from the Society, largely, one suspects, because the missionaries tended to cooperate in putting his case in a bad light to the Bishop.

The spectacle of two Anglican ministers suing one another for slander in a civil court in consequence of the alleged illegality of ecclesiastical court proceedings must have diverted the other religious bodies, and it was also a grave symptom of the appalling disunity that existed amongst the clergy. Of course, parsons occasionally squabbled in this way in England, but there was at hand an Archdeacon, or an Ordinary, to knock their heads together and force them to compromise their differences. In America these little differences produced scandalous rifts between two parsons, with the whole community joining in on one side or another. It was just another consequence of trying to have, in the colonies, an Episcopal church with Episcopacy left out. Not only the aggravation of these divisions, but the divisions themselves were due to lack of supervision by a Bishop, for a great many of them arose out of immorality either committed, or said to be committed by a clergyman. A Bishop could have tried these causes on the spot, and either deposed a defender if he were guilty, or cleared him in the eyes of the community if innocent. Anglican parsons were sworn, at the time of their ordaining, to live discreetly and religiously, but no one had ever tried the experiment of merely leaving them to their own devices and hoping for the best except in America, and there the consequences were disastrous.

The situation had an exact parallel in the realm of civil government. In colonial Newfoundland, the British Governor had appointed justices of the peace. These gradually died out; in consequence, when a murder was committed, there was no one to take cognizance of the offense. A trial might be held in England, but who would wish to go to England at his own expense in order to testify as a witness? The point that the American clergy broke out into excesses as a result of lack of government is well made by John Holt, who told the Bishop: "I have done all in my power to serve its [the Church's] interests, and maintain the clergy in their due credit and esteem, but unless I had a power to remove such as are notoriously scandalous in their lives, I cannot do effective service. I am sorry that I am under a necessity to inform your Lordship that there are many such here, and that I believe nothing will reclaim some of them until they feel the severity of ecclesiastical censures."[24] Holt knew what he was talking about, for he had made the acquaintance of some of the less desirable clerics. He says of one of them: "The last gentleman, Mr. Baily, is a very unhappy person, who, though his behaviour is far from being commendable, yet as he has received Holy Orders, I could not see him want bread (which he had thrown away upon some distaste to my parishioners) and I have again presented him to another parish, in hopes he will reform and become a new man."[25]

The Anglican clergy were the best friends King George had in America, but they were powerless to muster the very strong forces of Loyalist sympathy that existed in America

24. 3/124. John Holt, Maryland, Sept. 6th, 1715.
25. 21?/194. Maryland, June 20th, 1717.

without a Bishop at their head. It is only necessary to think
of the part played by the Anglican clergy as inspirers of the
Cavalier cause in the English civil war, and reflect on how
that inspiration was directed by the Bishops, to see how
disoriented the parsons were in 1776—soldiers without an
officer. The Great Rebellion in England had not been won
by the parsons' side, admittedly, but they had at least
achieved a moral defeat of the enemy, a result that they
largely owed to the episcopate, one of whom had produced
in the *Eikon Basilike*, a book of prayers allegedly written by
Charles I, one of the most effective pieces of propaganda
every written. If there had been a Bishop in America before
the Revolution, some connection with England might well
have been maintained. George the Third was to be obliged
to bite on the hard saying of a predecessor of his: "No
Bishop—No King."

In order to see just how difficult it was to administer the
American church from Britain, it is only necessary to read
the following extracts from letters and then ask oneself,
with the Bishop, "Who was in the right?"

"My Lord Mr. Campbell, a missionary appointed for the
ministry at Apoquiniminy having some differences with his
parishioners, I thought myself obliged to enquire. His conduct has not been so guarded and discreet as were to be
wished, his giving any handle to those that may be too
willing to magnify and set in the worst light, any failing of
the clergy (whom I honour) in an unjustifiable fault, and his
want of circumspection very blameable."[26]

"I understand [it is Campbell, the accused, who is speaking now] that through the clamour and noise of some of my
parishioners some missionaries met and were to represent
me in a very bad light. My Lord it is an unheard of thing that

26. Pennsylvania Box.

a man should be condemned unheard when he could have no access to vindicate himself, being at the time of their meeting under a fever and ague. My Lord, I plead a point of the Law of Nature, and I adjure your Lordship that I am heard before my adversaries face to face. If a man is condemned in his absence then whoever calumniates strongly will be sure to carry his point.

"My Lord I have done more for the Church of England since I came to this country than any two of those who have signed the report. My Lord, dont believe me upon my bare word, but suspend your judgement till the next ship arrives from this country, and then you'll see all I say attested by [the] whole congregation, and by gentlemen of candour and honour."[27]

More scandalous still, and not less instructive, was the case of Mr. Philipps, who was accused of "incest" because of alleged adultery with the wife and daughter of one of his parishioners. Apart from the fact that it allows the reader to savor the clerical invective of the period, it is interesting in that it throws light on the life of the white slaves of colonial America, the indentured servants, those poor wretches whose treatment in the North, in many instances, took from that part of America the right to criticize the servitude of the African toilers in the fields, which was often milder. At the same time there was this to be said for being an indentured servant in America, that the indentures would run out eventually, whereas in Scotland, for instance, one of the most democratic countries in Europe, little pockets of colliery bondslaves still existed, forgotten by the outside world, which was wont to assert that serfdom had died out in Scotland in the Middle Ages, and after a life of servitude carried the collar round their necks with them to the grave.

27. 9/56. Alexander Campbell, September 20th, 1727. Apoquiminy?

The indentured servant in this case, Elizabeth Starkey, plumbs the depths of degradation by being sold by her master after she had acted a very ambivalent part in the Philipps affair. The sadness of this part of our story is, however, offset by a gleam of light, the news of the fate of one of the surviving English highwaymen, who, retired from the road, had become an American politician. One wonders how many of his colleagues followed him across the Atlantic, into the same trade, in their retirement; it was better than gnawing cabbage stalks in Covent Garden.

In the case of Mr. Philipps, we shall hear, first of all, the churchwardens of Christ Church, Philadelphia. "The unchristian and barbarous treatment the reverend Mr. Philipps, our worthy minister, has met with, from Mr. John Moore, his Majesty's Collector of the Customs, and Mr. William Trent, a merchant in this city, grounded on some scandalous insinuations that appear altogether designing, false, and malicious, upon due impartial consideration, obliges us in behalf of ourselves and above three parts of a numerous congregation to renew and confirm our former good character of Mr. Philips, and also to acquaint your Lordship that no minister is or can be, more acceptable and serviceable to us."[28]

Parson Philipps now takes up his own defense. "One who goes by the name of John Smith, a notorious Roman Catholic, having been obliged in King William's reign to leave England and remove incognito into these parts for drinking confusion and damnation to the Prince, his Council, and Parliament, for which reason too, he thought it necessary to change his name from that of Bright to Smith. That can be proved. Upon a check given him by me, for using too familiar conversation with the man's wife in whose

28. 9/ no number. May 14th, 1715.

house he has resided, and for his customary and profane swearing and ridiculing our holy religion, swore he'd be revenged on me, and in order to put his wicked design in execution consults with one Jones, how they might ruin my interest and reputation amongst the people. 'Come,' says Jones, 'You and I will inform Mr. Moore that he was familiar with his daughter, and by that means we shan't only effect our design, but get money into the bargain, for Moore hates him.' 'This,' answers Smith, Is a good thought, but we must bring in somebody else otherwise the people will say that 'tis all spite and malice. Therefore,' adds Smith, 'We will bring in Mr. Trent, who is seemingly his friend.' John Moore sent Mr. Trent a letter to inform him that he had good evidence to prove that I had said that I had frequently lain with his wife and his daughter at the house of one Mr. Newman, his wife being privy to the whole intrigue, (all which, and every part of it she's ready to confute upon oath.)"[29]

The sudden and dramatic arrest of Philipps by the sheriff and his officers now followed. One of these officers, the retired highwayman referred to above, is described as "one Jones, that keeps a public house in this city. A fellow of the worst character and principle. [He] was accused of robbing on the highway before he left England, and if he had been catched, had undoubtedly been hanged."[30] The sheriff, Peter Evans, himself, according to Philipps, "is a person that has been accused of living in an open state of adultery with several persons ever since he came into ye country, particularly with one Grace's wife, whom he has lately prevailed with to swear that I had offerred to force her, though I have not been in her company these nine or ten months, and that

29. 9/13.
30. 9/37. Philadelphia, March 31st, 1715.

never but twice, once by accident and the first time by invitation." The Sheriff "has been suspended for packing juries, and the night before I met with such barbarous treatment, sent me a challenge written with his own hand without the least provocation. By this ill man (though at the time in a very [poor] state of health) I was dragged to gaol between eleven and twelve of the clock on Saturday night, January the twenty second, 1714, where I was detained till five in the afternoon on Sunday, and denied not only the civility of being admitted to stay in the undersheriff's house, but the liberty of sending for bail."[31]

We have already observed someone else sending a challenge to a duel to his minister, but nevertheless, this cannot be classed as anything other than a most unusual proceeding. Parsons were not supposed to cross swords like ordinary laymen because the clergy must not shed blood; canon law had been quite explicit on this point, and when fighting was really necessary, medieval churchmen had faithfully observed this injunction by carrying maces when going into battle. In the eighteenth century literary sources hint that parsons still issued challenges, even if they did not actually fight duels. There is a good story about one divinity graduate who had been promised a living by a college chum of his, who was the patron. Once he left the university, however, the patron changed his mind, and wanted to give the living to someone else. The parson promptly sent him a challenge. After a sleepless night the patron, who was no duelist, came to the parson in the morning and apologized for altering his mind about the benefice, whereupon the clergyman withdrew his challenge, protesting that he could not dream of endangering his benefactor's life. On the whole, though, it was a cowardly thing to send a clergyman a

31. *Ibid.*

challenge, for if he refused it might be for conscientious reasons, while if he accepted he would almost certainly find himself in trouble, not only with his ordinary, but with the civil authorities. The challenge sent to Parson Philipps by Sheriff Evans is, then something of a curiosity. It runs as follows:

Sir,
        You have basely scandalised a gentlewoman that I have a profound respect for. And for my part [I] shall give you a fair opportunity to defend yourself tomorrow morning on the west side of Josia Carpenter's garden betwixt seven and eight, where I shall expect to meet you *gladio cinctus*.[32] In failure whereof depend upon the usage you deserve from,

Yours etc.
Peter Evans

January ye 21st, 1714.
1 A.M. at ye Pewter Platter.[33]

The Sheriff is particular to put down the time of the early morning in which he was writing his challenge, because it was part of the duelist's code that a gentleman's honor was such a sacred thing that no possible delay should intervene between a fancied stain upon it and the exchange of bullets or sword thrusts that would wipe that stain out. Hence, besides giving the usual date on a letter of the time, the principals in a duel, when writing to one another, never failed to note down what time of day it was, thus showing that they were all impatience for the combat.

At this point the indentured servant, Elizabeth Starkey, one of those young women whose names were to be so frequently bandied about in this business makes her appearance. "William Moore and Trent," remarked Philipps, "and their instruments both of the clergy and laity, found

32. Girded with a sword.
33. 9/65. A.M. at ye Pewter Platter.

they could not accomplish their design by their malicious spreading their first accusations and adding as much more of pretended hearsay stuff as the father of discord could furnish 'em with. One Elizabeth Starkey, an impudent strumpet, is brought upon the stage. She was a servant to [Humphreys] whilst I boarded in his house, and had a bastard child by a sailor and was sold by Mr. Humphris to one Hawkins in the country."[34]

It is extraordinary that the literary legend of the beautiful forced emigrant should be confined to France and Manon Lescaut when Great Britain shipped so many more emigrants abroad, especially when the Revolution brought about the founding of Australia as a new convict colony. Like so many of these poor girls who were sent abroad in the eighteenth and nineteenth centuries, often for, in the first half of the period, some grave crime such as stealing sixpence or breaking the boughs of apple trees, Elizabeth was seduced by a sailor on the ship that brought her, as the following deposition sets out.

> Elizabeth Starkey, spinster, deposeth and sayeth that she is at present with child of a bastard child begotten upon her body by one John Philips, foremast man belonging to the ship *Hopewell* of Mynhead, whereof John Townshend was master, in which vessel she came a servant from England.
>
> Eigth day of February, 1713.
>
> The mark of Elizabeth Starkey.[35]

She now accused Philipps (whether on some quibble in the oath, such as that he had the same name as her seducer or not is difficult to say) of being the father of her child, only

34. 9/167. June 17th, 1714.
35. 9/168.

to retract the accusation afterwards, in some very revealing statements.

Philipps had been boarding with Humphreys, another Anglican clergyman but not a missionary, unless he was that John Humphrey of Trinity College Dublin, who had been incumbent at Oxford, and was now in Chester. It is in the house of Parson Humphreys that our next scene is set.

"Elizabeth Starkey, formerly, the servant of the Reverend Mr. Humphreys being sworn, deposed and saith that she was present when the said Mr. Humphreys and his wife with a hammer forced open a box of candles of Mr. Philip's and took out of the same box about seven or eight pound of candles and then nailed the box up again. And at the same time they opened a box of rice of the said Mr. Philipps and took out thence a little pillow beer[36] and nailed it again. And that a little before last Christmas her mistress, having the keeping of a cask of wine of Mr. Philipps, she drew out of the said cask four bottles and carried 'em into her own closet upstairs. And the deponent further saith that when Mr. Ashton sent for her to father her child, her Mistress was very angry and told this deponent it was Mr. Philipps' doing, and though she had not been here long enough to lay her child to him she might do him as great a diskindness, for he had an ill report at York. Upon Mr. Philipps and her mistress having words, her mistress said Mr. Philipps was fitter for a hangman than a minister. A little while after her mistress told this deponent she was with child; that she would murder it and be hanged, but Mr. Philipps had interest enough with the doctors to get stuff to murder it privately."[37]

36. Pillow case.
37. 9/134. July 1714.

A Philadelphia lady deposed as follows: "Elizabeth Starkey, formerly the servant of Mr. Humphreys, coming to her house the day before she was cried by John Hawkins her pretended master, going upstairs and being alone in company with the said Elizabeth Starkey, this deponent asked her several questions, viz. Whether she knew any ill thing of Mr. Philipps? To which she answered, No. That Mr. Philipps was a very civil gentleman and that he never offered an ill thing to her in his life, or so much as kissed her lips, and that she believed he scorned to touch such a one as she was, but, she added that her wicked mistress used all the means she could to make her swear against Mr. Philipps and father her child upon him, but that her conscience would not suffer her to do it. And then this deponent told her that 'twas reported that Mr. Philipps kept her a horse and side saddle, and gave her fine shifts and clothes, a furbelowed scarf, etc. To which Elizabeth Starkey answered that Mr. Philipps never gave her anything but an old gown, and that she had no shifts but some Ossembrigg[38] shifts, of which she had then two upon her back."[39]

Another matron from Philadelphia testified that "Being in company with Elizabeth Starky, and seeing her very uneasy and crying, this deponent asked her what was the matter, and she answered that Mr. Humphreys, or his wife, had sent her up word that they had got Mr. Philipps in prison and that they would have her in the pillory."

Nobody who had heard, and who was prepared to believe, that the wife of Parson Humphreys had broken into her lodger's supplies of provisions, conspired against him with her husband, although he was a parson of the same denomination as themselves, and then persuaded the ser-

38. Osnaburg.
39. 9/134. July 1714.

vant girl to get an abortive draught from Mr. Philipps, was likely to feel very keen either to join the Anglican church in Philadelphia or perhaps even to remain in it. In fact, if one believed the Humphreys and agreed with them that Philipps had been committing "incest" (cohabitation with two closely related women) with two of his parishioners, that hardly made things any better.

Obviously conduct, or suspected conduct of this sort, made the work of conversion much more difficult for the Episcopalians in America. It is true that they were no worse than the mother church at home, but there were other contemporary churches, also represented in America, that had retained a firmer hold on spiritual values than many of the parsons. Indeed, the history of some of the American parsons illustrates that it is not enough to belong to a church that possesses enormous worldly resources and to rely on home organization, a good supply of devotional literature, schools and colleges devoted to the propagation of a particular religious view, state support, and the like. The Anglican church in America was perhaps the best placed of all the churches for a total conversion of the whole of the American colonies. That it did not effect this may in part be put down to the excessive worldliness of some of its members. This was realized by many of the clergymen themselves, one of whom lamented, "The church of Philadelphia seems to languish at present for want of an established minister whose prudence and discretion might lead him to gain upon the multitude of various opinions dissenting from the church amongst us, as well as to unite more firmly together the members of that Communion themselves."[40]

Having said so much about the bad clergy, I must hasten to say that there were very many good ones as well, as the

40. 9/25.

occasional petitions on their behalf from their parishioners testify. Apart from these petitions, however, there is little evidence about them in this book, simply because they were not the type of persons to be mentioned in a letter to the Bishop. Besides petitions, testimonials help us to picutre the good minister who, exceptionally, is mentioned in this correspondence. "We whose names are hereunto subscribed, inhabitants of the township of Londonderry and adjacent parts, in the county of Chester and province of Pensilvania, do hereby certify that the reverend John Gordon did for the space of six years and a half lately past take care of the congregation belonging to John's church bordering on Fagg's Manor, with great care and diligence, and did during that time and doth still (as we verily believe) behave with strict virtue, sobriety, and honesty, to all people he was in any manner concerned with."[41]

The provenance of the S.P.G. missionaries to America at this time is a very interesting one. Of the clergy of the Western Shore in Maryland in 1723, four were Scots, two Irish, two Lancashire men, and one from Warwickshire, Derbyshire, Kent, and Northumberland respectively, while their commissary, Jacob Henderson, was an Irishman.[42] These figures were probably representative of the period as a whole. "To Ireland we owe several very choice missionaries," said a report,[43] and the official history remarks that "While the English universities failed to furnish a due supply of clergy for foreign service, Scotland, Ireland, and Wales were forward in contributing to the ranks of labourers."[44] The reason for this Celtic predominance among the

41. Pennsylvania Box/11.
42. 21/99.
43. Pascoe, p. 840.
44. *Ibid*.

missionaries is not difficult to explain. Wales and Ireland were both poor countries, with poor churches, and in Ireland, as Swift is never tired of telling us, all the best places were kept for Englishmen.

In Scotland it was illegal to say the English service, and anyone who attempted to do so was likely to be thrown into the local "Tolbooth" or jail. Irish, Welsh, and Scots, then, went to America because they probably could not find cures at home, while Englishmen tended to stay at home because they could, the Anglican church in England, Wales, and Ireland being presumably able to absorb most of the English who were ordained. Another category of Celt that came to America was the Huguenot parson, usually to minister to a French-speaking congregation, such as La Pierre, for example. Just how unwilling some Englishmen were to go to America as missionaries can be seen from the fact that a number of them drew money on the understanding that they were going out to the American colonies to minister there, but in fact stayed in England all their lives. Sir Leolyne Jenkyns had founded two fellowships at Jesus College, Oxford (England), by his will, in November 1685. The holders of these fellowships were bound to take holy orders and afterwards to go to sea as a Navy chaplain if summoned by the Lord High Admiral of England, or, if not required for that service, then to the Colonies, if called upon by the Bishop of London.[45] One of them did go, Henry Nicols, whom we have already met in Maryland. He noted on the questionnaire that his purpose on coming to Maryland "was to fulfill a condition on a fellowship, founded by Sir Leolin Jenkins in Jesus College in Oxon. I was first sent into Pensilvania by Bishop Compton, and by his persuasion removed here."[46] Nicols's election was formally notified to

45. Pascoe, p. 840.
46. 25/15

the Bishop, but he was the only fellow who ever went overseas. The rest stayed in Oxford; the Bishop may have called them, but they never came.

The fact that it was difficult for these non-English clerics to get jobs at home probably resulted in America's getting some good parsons. A Scottish Episcopalian minister might be a good churchman in every way, and have as his only disadvantage the fact that he could not get a post in Scotland, which was controlled by the Presbyterians, or England, where English parsons were preferred. At the same time, this prevailing non-English character of the parsons need not necessarily have made them more acceptable to the Americans, who were prepared to accept foreigners as foreigners, German, for instance, but who often exhibit a preference for English people when dealing with immigrants from the British Isles during this period. One has only to think of the continuous gibes at the Scotch-Irish at the time to see the force of this.

Besides these people, who came to America because they could not be accommodated with cures at home, parsons came out for a great variety of reasons, or talked about coming out to settle as a minister. A missionary mentions "One Mr. Hagar, a clergyman in the possession of one or two little livings in the diocese of Lincoln, and late chaplain to one of the regiments in Germany," who "came out of curiosity to see this town," and who subsequently preached in St. Pauls.[47]

It was always difficult to procure, in America, enough parsons to make ministering an easy matter, as the great shortage of curates showed. Thus in 1767, of the twenty-one New Jersey churches, eleven were without a minister, and there were only five clergymen to serve the remaining

47. 9/32. Philadelphia, November 14th, 1766.

ten. The Governor of North Carolina reported in 1764 that there were six clergymen between twenty-nine parishes, each of which consisted of a whole county.[48] This shortage of parsons was chiefly due to the remoteness of America, and the vagueness of the ideas people entertained about it (ministers in their letters refer to it in such terms as "these remote parts") and the great danger of crossing the Atlantic. One in five of those who began the voyage died before reaching their cures.[49] The fatal history of the incumbents of Hebron, in Connecticut, is worth remembering in this respect. Hebron sent to England, for ordination, first of all Mr. Dean, in 1745, who died at sea on the voyage back; then Mr. Colton, who died of smallpox, caught on the return voyage in 1752; then Mr. Usher, who suffered the nameless horrors of a French prison before dying of disease in Bayonne in 1757. The last of the American candidates, Mr. Peters, also caught smallpox, but recovered and got back to Hebron.

The courage of the American ordinands, most of them second-generation Americans, and some of them representatives of American clergymen's families, who put out year after year to get their orders in England would have ennobled any cause, and it is not surprising to find them, to quote Pascoe "the ablest of the missionaries." The sacrifice was not only one of youth. The parents of these boys must have sighed bitterly when they committed their Benjamins to the perils of the Atlantic. In parsons' families the struggle with oneself, before going to England, must have been even greater, for clergymen's sons had heard from their fathers of their own experience of the voyage. At the best it would be a year or more before the ordinands could come back.

48. Pascoe, p. 841.
49. Pascoe, p. 840.

Mail delivery was very bad, and nothing might be heard for months from the absent ones. "Above twenty missions," wrote a parson, "are now vacant. It is considered that a thousand pounds will not be sufficient to pay for the voyage and expenses attending the ordination of twenty missionaries. Such a sum, great as it is, is but a trifle in comparison to loss of time, risks at sea, and other discouragements, which frighten many well disposed persons, and set parents and relations against the first motions that might arise towards the ministry in our church, whilst hundreds of dissenting preachers can be made with but little expense, and forthwith dispatched to any part of the continent, where the Synod wants either to supply settled places or open new ones."[50]

If the churchwardens of a parish did not have an ordinand to send abroad, the usual procedure was either to write to the Bishop, asking him to send out a parson, or perhaps to write to a prospective parson emigrant and give him a call. This call would take a form like the following:

Sir,
    We are informed by Mr. William Gale of your worth, and that there are hopes you may be induced to come abroad into this part of the world, which makes us (as vestry men) give you the trouble of this to acquaint you that the parish aforesaid though worth 20,000 pounds of tobacco a year to a minister, besides his perquisites, for marriages, funeral sermons, etc., and is daily increasing, is now without a minister, and if you'll favour us so far as to come over here and accept it, this shall oblige us to present you to our governor for induction.[51]

If, on the other hand, the parish had an ordinand in

50. 9/32. Philadelphia, November 14th, 1766.
51. 3/206. Vestry of Somerset County in Maryland, June 31st, 1721.

hand, and he was being presented to the bishop for ordination, the letter of introduction would run somewhat like this.

> The need that I and my parish stand in of a curate hath emboldened me to trouble your Lordship in behalf of the bearer, Mr. Nathaniel Whitaker, who by sundry private letters from gentlemen of the clergy in New England together with his public testimonials, discreet and Christian behaviour since he came to this province, which has been the space of ten months, gives me great reason with submission to presume that your Lordship will find the young gentleman qualified for holy orders, and that he may obtain your Lordship's licence to officiate in [a] ministerial function in this Province.[52]

The writer of the letter, Thomas Fletcher, remarked in addition that his congregation was falling off because they found it difficult to get to church. A curate would probably have held them together by going out to preach in a chapel in the outlying parts of the parish. This was an experience probably shared by other American parsons.

An American parson would, of course, write to the Bishop on behalf of his son, if he were sending him across for ordination. Here is an heroic American father writing for this purpose. I use the word *heroic* advisedly, because the writer of the letter, George Ross, missionary at Newcastle and Chester, had been a prisoner in France, almost contemporary with the Cordiners, in 1711. He therefore knew what might happen to his son George. Nevertheless, he did not dissuade him when he expressed a wish to go into the church. "Having narrowly inspected into my son's genius, and natural disposition and finding him upon all occasions virtuously inclined and fond of learning. I gave way to his inclination and cherished his bent to serve the church. He

---

52. 21?/193. Thomas Fletcher, Maryland, Somerset County, June 18th, 1740.

now waits upon your Lordship, with such ample credentials as, I hope will give your Lordship full satisfaction as to the integrity of his life."[53] Aeneas Ross's trust in the Almighty was justified, for George Ross came back and ministered for more than forty years as a missionary in Philadelphia, Oxford, Whitemarsh, and his father's old parish.

All sorts of unlikely persons suddenly took it into their heads to become ministers, the strangest instance being that of an actor playing comedy parts in a touring company. Lord Baltimore wrote to the Bishop on behalf of a Mr. Chaff, who had been intended for a lawyer, mentioning that "he has had a liberal education and as he is very conversant in law, I hope he will not only be of credit to the clergy in his ecclesiastical function, but of service to them in his advice when their property is concerned."[54] These sudden demands for orders need not be put down to mere opportunism; America was the land of sudden religious conversions, and there were abundant exhorters at hand to put men in mind of God, if their mere environment, their remoteness from Europe, the desert land in which they found themselves, and the imminence of attack by the Indians or the French or Spaniards did not do so.

It will have been noticed that some American ordinands left for England at an early age, so as to go to school in England and improve their Greek and Latin, difficult to acquire in the colonies, and bring those subjects up to the rather slender attainments of graduates in the English universities who were also going to be ordained. Next to the want of a Bishop in America, the principal hindrance to

53. The careers of the two Rosses are given in Pascoe, p. 852. Ross the elder was, significantly a Nonjuror. Was he also a Scottish Highlander, and therefore an enemy of Alexander Campbell, whose opponent he was, and who was a representative of the much more successful clan of Campbell, which had achieved a dominant position in the Highlands at this time, and was hated accordingly?
54. 3/205.

church work in the colonies had been the lack of a university that would also act as a church seminary for Anglican parsons. Those Anglicans who had gone to Nonconformist universities had been obliged in some instances "to submit to a fine as often as they attended the worship of the Church of England, communicants only excepted and those only on Sacrament days."[55] This need for a seminary was met with the foundation of Kings College, now Columbia University, New York. An interesting relic of this first Anglican seminary in America, and of the American ordinands in England, is the graduation parchment of one of the first classmen in the first class of King's College, one of the first American Bishops, who was also perhaps the last American ordinand.

The date of the parchment is June the third, 1761, and it belonged to one of the men in the first class Columbia University (then King's College) sent out. This class in 1754 began their studies eight strong, but only five graduated in 1758. The document runs as follows:

Praeses Collegii Regis, quod est Novi Eboraci in America, regio diplomate constituti; ex jussu honoratissimorum eiusdem Collegii Regentium omnibus Christfidelibus, ad quos hae literae presentes pervenerint, salutem in Domino sempiternam. Vobis notum sit, quod Samuelem Provost, optimae spei juvenem hujus collegii nuper ab initio alumnum, qui probe se gesserat, omniaque studia et exercitia, legibus praescripta perfecerat, atque ad Baccalaureatis in Artibus Gradum tribus abhinc annis, provectus fuerat, at probavimus quam approbavimus, atque unanimi consensu; ad Magistratus in Artibus Gradum iam denuo proveximus, eumque omnibus juribus et privilegiis ad istum gradum attinentibus ornavimus. In cuius rei majorem fidem et plenius testimonium sigillum

55. Pascoe, p. 841.

commune nostrum quo hac in parte utimur praesentibus apponi fecimus; Datis ex hujusve Collegii Aula, die mensis Junii tertio, Annoque Domini millesimo Septingentesimo Sexagesimo primo.

Samuel Johnson . . .

The diploma, which is endorsed "Mr. Provost," may be here accompanied by a translation:

The Head of King's College, which is in New York in America, constituted by royal charter, on the order of the most honourable Regents of the same college to all faithful Christians to whom these present letters may come. Continual greetings in the Lord.

May it be known to you that Samuel Provost, a young man of the highest promise, who was till recently a student of this college, from its beginning and who has behaved himself fittingly and carried out all the studies and exercises prescribed by the laws, and who, three years since, was advanced to the degree of Bachelor of Arts, has been tested and approved of by us, and with the consent of all we have now advanced him once again, to the degree of Master of Arts, and have honoured him with all the rights and privileges pertaining to this degree.

For the greater credit and fuller testimony of which we have ordered our common seal, which we use for this purpose, to be attached to the presents. Given in the hall of this college, the 3rd of June 1761.

Samuel Johnson . . .

The seal in question was presented by Mr. George Harding, who paid £10 for the engraving. The matrix for the seal on Provost's parchment was lost or stolen during the inches. Pink ribbons, tied at the end with a twist of thread, attach it though the seal is in fine condition, and the definition of the impression very good, I was glad to be able to collate my reading of the very minute inscription with the official account of the device.[56] This is as follows:

> The College is represented by a lady sitting in a throne or chair of state, with several children at her knee to represent the pupils, with 1. Peter II, 2, 7v. under them to express the temper with which they should apply themselves to seek true wisdom. The words are: "Wherefore laying aside all malice and all guile, and hypocrisies and envies and evil speakings, as new born babes desire the sincere milk of the Word, that ye may grow thereby, etc. One of them she takes by the hand with her left hand expressing her benevolent design of conducting them to true wisdom and virtue. To which purpose she holds open to them a book in her right hand in which is [in] Greek letters the living or lively oracles, which is the epithet that St. Stephen gives to the Holy Scriptures, Acts 7, 38. Out of her mouth over her left shoulder goes a label with these words in Hebrew letters, ORI, EL, "God is my light," alluding to Ps. 27: 1, expressing her acknowledgment. Mal. iv. 2., The sun of righteousness arising with healing in his wings. Over her head is Jehovah in a glory, the beams coming triangularly to a point near her head, with these words around her for her motto. "In lumine tuo videbimus lumen." In thy light shall we see light. Psal. 36, 9. On the edge round are engraved in capitals: SIGILLUM COLLEGII REG. NOV. EBOR. IN AMERICA.

The seal in question was presented by Mr. George Harding, who paid L 10 for the engraving. The matrix for the seal on Provost's parchment was lost or stolen during the American War of Independence, and it was not until 1914 that it reappeared at Williamsport, Pennsylvania, in the hands of a private individual, shortly after which time it was returned to the University.

While the seal of the document is by no means unique, it seems that the graduation parchment is. None of the origi-

56. A History of Columbia University, 1754-1904, by members of the staff (London, 1904).

nal class of seven who received their B.A. in 1758 were given diplomas. President Samuel Johnson placed a small Hebrew psalter, still kept in the library, in the hand of the graduate, and conferred the degree with a Latin formula. In 1759 Samuel Verplanck, one of the class, apparently wanted written evidence of his degree, and he was given a written diploma stating, in Latin, that he had received the degree of B.A. in 1758. There are no other diplomas for the presidency of Samuel Johnson, and therefore Provoost's diploma is one of the two he issued, and is the only M.A. diploma for King's College during the presidency of its founder president. Incidentally, it is the only really early diploma for King's College (except Verplanck's) that issued from the hands of a scrivener, the later ones, given by Miles Cooper, the second president, being engraved on copper.

The circumstances of the parchment's having come to Lambeth are scarcely less remarkable. Provoost was one of the Bishops elected in America and sent over for ordination after the American Episcopacy had been inaugurated by the conferring of consecration upon Seabury by the Aberdeen Nonjurors. The archbishops and Bishops were asked that "from a tender regard to the religious interests of thousands in this rising empire, professing the same religious principles with the Church of England, you will be pleased to confer the Episcopal character on such persons as shall be recommended by this Church in the several states here represented: Full satisfaction being given of the sufficiency of the persons recommended."[57]   It is owing to this offer of "full satisfaction," and its acceptance, that the parchment came to rest among the Lambeth miscellanea. It

57. I am indebted to Mr. M. Halsey Thomas, Curator of Columbiana at Columbia University, for giving me a good deal of the information used in this section. See Hugh G.G. Herklot, *The Church of England and the American Episcopal Church* (London: A.R. Mowbray & Co. Ltd., 1966), p. 100.

must have been produced and exhibited to the Archbishop's lawyers previous to Provoost's consecration, in Lambeth Palace Chapel on February 4, 1787, and left in the Palace, as much out of place in that English background as the Red Indians who stand guard forever beside the tablet commemorating the young American killed while reconnoitering Ticonderoga, which stands in the aisles of Westminster Abbey.

6

"A Strange Sort of Church Indeed!"

So far we have heard very little about what is not the least important part of a church—the congregation. This is because the parsons were less interested, when they came to write to the Bishop, in their flock than in other parsons. Those glimpses which we obtain of the folk in the body of the kirk, though fascinating, are tantalizingly brief. Here, for example, is a testimonial to a young layman that has strayed into the collection, as it were by accident.

To the worthy Madam Lane, John Eversfield, having been well recommended to me as a youth of good learning and pious education, and of an ingenuous, sober, and honest behaviour and deportment, was by me employed to write at my seat in the six clerks' office for one year or thereabouts. During all which time he behaved himself faithfully and honestly in everything committed to his trust or under his care and was careful and diligent in whatever he was to do in my service, and was become capable of getting a competent livelihood in the said office, until he received a blow or bruise on his right elbow, from Mr. Thomas Lane deceased as I have been credibly informed by which means he has lost his right arm, and thereby rendered uncapable of writing or any other manual employment, whereby to live and he, being an orphan and having no manner of worldly substance to support him, or relations to rely on for relief, he then was and still is fit to be recommended to the charity of all well disposed people.[1]

There is something characteristically American in the placing of the onus of relief for this poor boy, not on the parish, but on the person most concerned with it, the widow of the man who had caused his disablement.

There is a chance reference to what was a very important part of life in the colonies, smuggling. "A ship called the *Fame* illegally imported to Philadelphia in the said province great quantities of East India and other contraband to the value of twenty thousand pounds and upwards, which ship and cargo the said collector [John Moore] did seize and secure in the best manner he could for his Majesty's use.

"The ship's crew, assisted by seventy or eighty persons in disguise in the night time, forced the ship, etc. out of the Collector's hands, and Sir William Keith, Deputy Governor of the said Province, cause a procedure to be made against the said ship and cargo in opposition to the Collector."[2]

The account given below shows how quickly even first-generation German immigrants adopted American folk ways, their courting patterns, for example. Susanna Maus, wife of Frederick Maus of Philadelphia, stocking weaver, deposed that: "Sometime in the month of August or September 1761 a certain man who called himself William Deadman came to her house in order, as she thought to see

1. 21/76. Matthew Osbourne.
2. 9/140. 1724.

her daughter Charlotte, a girl then about sixteen years of age. That after the said Deadman had been at her house two or three times, she became very uneasy on account of her said daughter Charlotte; the said Deadman appeared a stranger. That she, this deponent, not speaking very good English, being a German, prevailed on one Mary Preistley her neighbour, to speak to the said Deadman in the name of her this deponent, and to know of him if he was a married or a single man, and what were his intentions in visiting her daughter, whether to play the fool with her and make a whore of her, or if he wanted to marry her. He declared that he never had been married, and that he came to see the said girl Charlotte in order to make her his wife. Very soon after the said Deadman asked of the said Frederick Maus the liberty of his house to court his said daughter. To which the said Maus at first agreed, but considering that the said Deadman was a stranger, he afterwards forbade him to come to his house. That the said Deadman, persisting to keep company with Charlotte and that continued to give her company to him, he the said Frederick Maus consented that his said daughter might be married, though he wished to have prevented it, and accordingly a day was fixed.

"Frederick Maus, soon after he had given his consent, as aforesaid went on a journey to Lancaster, and that during his absence the said Susanna and Frances these deponents as well as other persons discovered that the said Deadman and Charlotte had been too free with each other, which occasioned great uneasiness in the family."

The story now continues, apparently in the mouth of Charlotte's married sister. "She this deponent being very uneasy in her mind respecting the situation of her sister Charlotte, purposely entered into a free conversation with the said Deadman and acquainted him that as he was a stranger she was afraid lest he might have a wife already, and therefore she entreated the said Deadman to declare if he was a single or a married man, adding that if he was married, notwithstanding the injury he had done her sister Charlotte, and disgraced the family, yet if he had a wife already, he should by no means be married to her sister. Upon which the said William Deadman solemnly protested that as sure as he wished to come to the Kingdom of Heaven he never knew what a married life was.

"Frances Maus further saith that she, having formerly lived with the Reverend Mr. William Sturgeon, assistant minister at Christ Church in Philadelphia aforesaid, and thereby being well acquainted with him, was desired by the said Deadman to ask if the said Mr. Sturgeon had any blank marriage licences, but he, answering in the negative, advised them to apply to the office, this being on the evening of the said twelfth day of October, and past office hours, the Clerk of the Office was not to be found, though he was sought for diligently at his lodgings and several other places, the said Mr. Sturgeon consented to marry the said William and Charlotte without a licence, as he Mr. Sturgeon then said, in order to restore this distressed family to their former ease and happiness."[3] Mr. Sturgeon got into trouble for his kindness, since the marriage was, of course, illegal.

The layman with whom a parson was likely to have his most important contacts, whether for weal or woe, was the royal governor. Often an incoming parson would have letters of introduction to present to him, as in the following case; if not, the Bishop would probably write on his behalf under separate cover.

"We arrived safe in Maryland, in the beginning of August last," wrote a parson, "and delivered your Grace's letter to his Excellency at Annapolis, who by this fleet doth return

3. 9/141.

his answer. I found him employed in erecting a statehouse for the administration of justice, a fine brick building in which are comprehended convenient apartments for all the offices of business in the country. This is almost finished. We are now going on with as fine a church, which will cost a thousand, his Excellency giving a hundred towards it, and a school at the same time."[4]

Not all colloquies between parson and governor were as friendly as this. We have seen how bitter a governor could become against a cleric if his politics were the opposite of his own—nonjuring, for example. Similarly, a governor determined to overturn his predecessor's policy, as some governors were, would find cause for complaint in a parson who had admired the last holder of the office, as in the case described below.

"The ninth of November, Sir Richard Everard came up to the house where I lived in Bertie precinct, where I had two days conference with Sir Richard in my own chamber, and Sir Richard's discourse being stuffed very much with unusual reflections on our late Governor, Mr. Burrington, I showed a dislike, whereupon Sir Richard took upon him to reflect upon myself by telling me that I not only stood precarious as a minister here, but that it was in his power to prevent me preaching here to the people. I humbly answered him that I had done nothing unbecoming my ministerial function, but had more diligently attended in the precinct than any other former minister. Upon which Sir Richard became more moderate but still levelling his discourse against Mr. Burrington, I expressed an uneasiness by telling him that I knew of no harm of Mr. Burrington and that I could not speak with other men's tongues, and I told Sir Richard, that if I could not obtain his

4. Maryland Box/192.

countenance without speaking evil of any man that I knew
no evil of, I must despair of obtaining it. Sir Richard then
was very calm and invited me and my wife to his house at
Edenton.

"Accordingly the Monday following I met with the Reverend Mr. Blackwell. I asked leave of his pulpit, he
answered, 'I was welcome to his pulpit.' Soon after I met
with Sir Richard's son [and] told him I intended to preach
tomorrow. He told me his father invited me to a dish of
chocolate in the morning. I answered I would wait upon Sir
Richard and accordingly did, where I met with a free access
[and] good entertainment, exceptions [being] only some
scandalous and gross reflections on Mr. Burrington. I told
Sir Richard I was not susceptible of such egregious reflections on a gentleman of so vast a character among rich and
poor. Immediately entered a bevy of ladies to breakfast with
Sir Richard, and the ladies to come to church at the time
appointed. And after I had taken a walk [of] about an hour
and [a] half, meeting with Mr. Pariss, he asked me whether
it was not time for church or no? I answered in the affirma-
tive, asking him, 'Who kept the key?' Who answered, 'Mr.
Badham, and that he would go for it,' and immediately did,
and as soon returned, telling me the Governor had sent for
it, at which I was very surprised. The congregation being
ready for their devotion, there was a great murmuring,
from which I understood that the door would be broke
open. I desired them not to do it, for I would go to Sir
Richard for the key myself rather than any violence should
be used. And accordingly I approached Sir Richard (who
was then in company with Doctor Min, a man of a vile
character, and lately condemned at Williamsburg for cursing King George and Mr. Drysdale, who is Governor of
Virginia) 'Sir Richard,' (I said) 'The congregation waits to

go to church, and I beg that your honour will please to let me have the key.'

"He, then taking the key then up, in a big rage, thus expressed himself. 'Sirrah I will make you know who is Governor!' I answered I knew that his honour was Governor and I hoped that his honour knew likewise who was priest. He replied I should not preach today. I told him that I would, and that unless his honour would please to send the key, I was assured by what I heard that the door would be opened. He said he would put me in prison if I did preach. I (said) however that I would try that, not doubting but that God would defend me. I then departed and came to Church where the door was open. I went in to read Divine Service, and gave the people a sermon. The next morning a warrant was sent by the Constable from Justice Gale. When I came before the Justice, he examining me, demanded security or would order me to prison. To prison I must have went had not Mr. Burrington's compassion and love to the clergy prevented me by offering himself bail, which was accepted."[5]

The time had now come, however, when the ministers, or a great many of them, were to come to grips with their congregations, or parts of those congregations. The parsons had been one of the mainstays of King George in America, and had opposed, as best they could, revolutionary principles. Samuel Johnson, the President of King's College, New York, and a representative of the more intellectual type of parson, had written thirteen years before revolution broke out: "Is there then nothing more that can be done, either for obtaining Bishops or demolishing these pernicious Charter Governments and reducing them all to

5. 10/37. Thomas Baylye, vera copia, 1725?.

one form in immediate dependance on the King? I can't help calling them *pernicious*, for they are indeed so, as well for the best good of the people themselves as to the interest of true religion."[6] While the clergy were largely loyalist, however, at least in the North, they could see, better than most, what a civil war would entail, and they had no particular desire to participate actively in one. A little finesse on the part of the revolutionaries would have rendered them, if not neutral, then inactive. As an indication of the Anglican desire to stand aside from the conflict, if that were possible, the following document is an interesting one.

At the annual meeting of our Corporation for the relief of the widows and children of clergymen in the Communion of the Church of England in America at Philadelphia, after the usual business was discussed the worthy clergy of this city communicated to those of their clerical brethern who were present, an address lately transmitted from them to your Lordship, giving a state of the difficulties under which the ministers of the Church of England in this country labour at this important crisis, informing your Lordship of the military associations which had taken place among all denominations throughout these colonies, and that in such a situation of affairs they considered it as a step of prudence on their part necessary to the continuance of their own usefulness and even to the preservation of our church in America, to comply with the recommendation of Congress and the request of their parishioners in observing the twentieth of July last, as a day of general humiliation, fasting and prayer. We desire to assure your Lordship and also our spiritual supervisors that on this occasion we did scrupulously conduct ourselves consistently with our duty as loyal subjects and ministers of the Church of England. Our distresses are great. Our anxiety for the welfare of the whole British Empire still greater, but in these most trying times we hope to approve ourselves the hearty and steady friends of the Constitution both in Church and State,

6. Letter from Samuel Johnson, Stratford, December 20th, 1763. L.P.L.

and the faithful ministers of the gospel of peace and love. But at the same time we think it of importance to the interest of our country at large to have it known that even were it proper for us to take any active part in the present troubles it would not be of any considerable weight on either side of that fatal dispute we so heartily wish to see happily accomodated.

We do most heartily join our brethren in the prayer contained in their letter. That the hearts of good and benevolent men in both countries may be directed to pursue such truly salutary measures as may produce a speedy and permanent reconciliation between the Mother Country and her colonies, and we humbly recommend ourselves to your Lordship's paternal prayers, advice, and protection.

> We are
> My Lord
> Your Lordship's dutiful sons and servants.

Philip Reading,
George Craig,
Thomas Barton,
Charles Inglis,
Alexander Murray,
Jonathan Odell,
Samuel Magaw,
William Thompson,
George Panton,
D. Batwell,
Samuel Tingley,
William Frayer.[7]

The names of those who signed this declaration are highly significant. All these people wished to be neutral at this point in the development of the Revolution. What was the eventual part they played in it?

Reading died during the war, possibly as a result of the hardships he endured in it, as so many missionaries did. He

7. 9/30. Philadelphia, October 6th, 1775. A corporation for the relief of the widows and children of clergymen in the provinces of New York, New Jersey, and Pennsylvania was established in 1769, the Society contributing £20 annually to each of the three branches.

describes the closing of his church in the following words: "After the Nicene Creed I declared, in form that as I had no design to resist the authority of the new Government on one hand, and as I was determined on the other, not to incur the heavy guilt of perjury by a breach of the most solemn promises, I should decline attending on the public worship for a short time from that day. I had purposed to say more on the subject, but the scene became too affecting for me to bear a further part in it. Many of the people present were overwhelmed with distress, and the cheeks of some began to be bathed in tears. My own tongue faltered and my firmness forsook me; beckoning therefore to the clerk to sing the psalm, I went up into the pulpit, and having exhorted the members of the church to "hold fast the profession of their faith without wavering," and to depend upon the promises of a faithful God for their present comfort and future relief, I finished this irksome business, and Apoquimininck Church from that day has continued shut up."[8]

Craig is not described by the official history as having been "persecuted" by the revolutionaries, but as the heroic Barton pointed out: "Every clergyman of the Church of England who dar'd to act upon proper principles was mark'd out for infamy and insult, in consequence of which the missionaries in particular have suffered greatly, been driven from the habitations and families, laid under arrests and imprisoned."[9] The unravaged condition of Barton's parishes during the French and Indian war had borne witness to his public spirit and bravery, but he had to close his churches, was a prisoner for two years and after he had escaped to the British lines, died there of a dropsy brought on by imprisonment. Inglis, the incumbent of Trinity, New

8. Pascoe, p. 39.
9. Pascoe, pp. 2, 39, 40, 851.

York, escaped and became the first colonial bishop. Murray was a refugee in England. Jonathan Odell's name is already probably well known to readers as the author of some spirited loyalist verses. He lay a prisoner among other Tories after being forced to abandon his church in Burlington, escaped through the revolutionary lines, became an army chaplain, and died in Frederickton, New Brunswick, after having seen his parishioners, the children of the Loyalists, build up a new, loyal American nation in Canada, and beat off an attack from old America. It is difficult to see what Samuel Magaw did during the war; perhaps, like Thompson, he threw in his lot with the revolutionaries. Batwell, like so many of the Loyalist refugees, went to New York and thence to England. Tingley, cut off from correspondence with the Society, watched his wife die, refused medicine by the revolutionary troops. There was no need, on the part of the revolution, to drive the parsons to these extremities. They would have stayed quiescent in their parishes if they had been allowed to pray for King George as the Anglican service prescribed. It is not irreverent to suggest that they could have done the rebel cause no harm by this, for the web of the British in America was already spun.

Rabbling the clergy in this way certainly did the patriots no good—atrocities can never benefit any cause—and it harmed them in that it drove the parsons and their families, and a good many of their congregations, into the arms of the British. It may have seemed clever to the revolutionaries to drive out so many Episcopalian families, and the clergymen were a tempting prey, being of course defenseless. From a long-term point of view, however, it was disastrous. The Loyalist families, having lost their Augustan culture in the woods of Canada, had nevertheless acquired the ability to shoot, as 1812 was to show. Just how determined the patriots were to force the Anglican ministers from their homes and churches can be seen by the following correspondence between the Rev. Haddon Smith and the revolutionary committee in Georgia, which has not been published before.

Haddon Smith, the rector of Savannah in Georgia, appeared before the Mayor of Liverpool and deposed that, some time back, the local patriots in Savannah had informed him that "a motion was made and seconded, that the Reverend Mr. Haddon Smith be required to preach a sermon on Thursday next, suitable to the present differences subsisting between Great Britain and the Colonies, on account of an order from the Continental Congress, for the inhabitants of the United Provinces to set apart that day for fasting and prayer and humiliating ourselves before Almighty God, the said Mr. Smith be required to preach a suitable sermon on that day." When notice of this decision had been served on Smith, he declined politely.

"I beg leave to remind you that his Excellency the Governor has appointed *Wednesday* next for a day of fasting, humiliation, and prayer to Almighty God on account of the unhappy differences at present subsisting between these colonies and the parent state, when I purpose to discharge the duties of my profession in obedience to that authority. Nothing hurts me more than being under the disagreeable necessity of refusing any thing that is politely requested of me, but as a clergyman of the Church of England, I think myself bound in conscience not to do anything of a public nature without the express authority of my lawful superior. I sincerely and ardently wish a reconciliation between us and our parent state and shall sincerely and heartily pray for it, but I must beg that you will excuse me in not complying with your request upon the present occasion."

The patriot reply to Smith was as follows.

"Sir,

"As you live in one of the associated provinces of North America it is but proper that you pay due regard to all the orders of the Continental Congress whose authority now pervades the whole, and as they have appointed Thursday the twentieth instant a day of fasting and prayer it is our duty and inclination to join in keeping that day sacred.

"We therefore must inform you that we think it neither will be decent or safe for you to stand in opposition to the people of this country and the united voice of America."

Smith ignored this, and on the twenty-second of July, a detachment of patriots waited on him and addressed him as follows. "From your late conduct in disobeying the orders of the Congress you are deemed an enemy to America; and by order of the Committee we are to inform you that you are to be suffered no longer to officiate in this town." Christ Church, Savannah, was then seized by the patriots, and a patriot clergyman put in, Edward Langworthy. According to Smith, he was lucky to have escaped with his life, for John Hopkins, a seaman who had been tarred and feathered by the patriot mob at the Dial in Savannah, after being forced to drink "Damnation to all Tories and success to American liberty." on the threat of being hung from the Liberty Tree ("Fat as I am," remarked one of the patriots, "I will get up and hang you myself."), was told that "if they could lay hold of the parson they would put him alongside of this deponent in the cart, that this deponent also heard said in the mob that 'Mr. Smith should be next.'"[10]

These scenes were repeated all over America. It is not correct to say, as W.W. Sweet does, that "the S.P.G. mis-

10. Georgia Box /82. Rev. Haddon Smith, rector of Savannah in Georgia, sworn copies given to the Mayor of Liverpool.

sionaries left the country almost to a man, at the opening of the war, leaving deserted the country parishes, outside Virginia and Maryland," for they were driven away by the patriots, as anyone who takes the trouble to read their individual histories in Pascoe will see for himself.

Thus ended the organized mission to America from the Anglican church. It is significant that unlike the Swedes or the Dutch, the English did not continue to help those of their national church who had passed under another government. Perhaps they felt that in view of the disestablishment of the Anglican churches that was beginning in America it was a risky thing to send money to help a church whose funds might be confiscated, or perhaps they hated the now independent Americans too much to wish them in heaven. This attitude was also observable in the refusal of the English Bishops to consecrate Seabury, who achieved consecration at the hands of the despised Nonjurors in Scotland, fellow communicants with those American Nonjurors who had led such worthy and persecuted lives in the colonies. At this bold step the resistance of the English Episcopate weakened. They were not going to allow the Nonjurors to be the only diocesans to consecrate American bishops, and the consecration of Provoost and White took place in Lambeth Palace Chapel. Provoost left for his new diocese the following day, having left his graduation parchment, the mark of his intellectual attainments, and the most precious possession of a scholar, in the hands of the Archbishop's officials (who lost it), without waiting to reclaim the document. Elsewhere I have interpreted this act as one of Godly haste, an urgent desire to be with his subjects, but could there not also have been too in this haste an element of impatience with the Erastian hierarchy, who had worked so much harm to the American Episcopalians?

It did not need an Act of Parliament to provide a Bishop

for Anglican America, as the S.P.G. and the episcopate continued to assert plaintively during the colonial period. If instead, one of the bench of Bishops had visited the colonies once, as Bishop Berkeley did, that would have been sufficient to confirm the young, ordain the ministers, and coerce ecclesiastical offenders, and this would have sufficed for the needs of the church. This action might have helped to stave off the rupture between America and Britain, and it would certainly have saved the lives of those young men, the flower of their country, who put out to England for ordination, only to find martyrdom at sea or in a French prison. And in the scale of spiritual values, how many Episcopalians had either never enjoyed, or died without the consolation of, their religion, due to this fatal neglect to provide a head of the church in America?

The American Episcopalians appeared to have lost all after the Revolution, but their loss in reality had been a small one. Many of their ministers had gone, but now that there was an American episcopate, it was possible to replace them without pouring out lives and money. Many of the most faithful Episcopalians had moved north or gone overseas, but others would, in abundance, fill the ranks of the church. Many of the Anglican churches had been taken from their congregations, but it is a mistake to think that a church is attached to its meeting place in the way that a tortoise is attached to its carapace. Most important of all, the British government had lost control of the direction of the American church; it was free now to work out its own salvation, free to recognize no one but Christ as its head, free to represent nothing but American Episcopalianism. The dream of some American Anglicans of the colonial period had been realized, and they had now "an independent Church of England." If it was better, as it could not fail to be, for that independence from the Church of England, still sunk in its immemorial sleep; if it was more representative of those early reformers who had shaped it in the sixteenth century—more like a church and not just a department of the state; then those rivers of blood which both sides had poured out in the Revolution would not have flowed in vain.

Select Bibliography

Manuscript Sources

The manuscript sources used for this book all come from Lambeth Palace Library. Apart from the narratives of Hesketh and Cordiner—which are referred to in their place in chapter II, all the manuscript sources are to be found in the Fulham Papers. During the seventeenth and eighteenth centuries the vague authority exercised by the Bishop of London over the colonial church resulted in many letters being sent by the clergy in the colonies to the bishop. Apart from the commissary, who was a regular correspondent, the Bishop of London might, as is seen, receive letters from a wide variety of people. During any crisis or controversy, the volume of his postbag from America would increase.

Most of the research work for this book was carried out prior to 1959, when the Fulham Papers were rearranged and catalogued. The system of indexing that I used in compiling the book, and that to which the references refer, is that which the Bishop of the day would have himself used. Professor W.W. Manross's catalogue: "The Fulham Papers in the Lambeth Palace Library. American Colonial Section. Calendar and Indexes. Oxford 1965" has two voluminous indexes that will help readers in referring from the old classification to the new.

Printed Books and Articles

Cross, Arthur L. *The Anglican Episcopate and the American Colonies*. New York: Green and Co., 1902.

Drummond, Andrew L. *The Story of American Protestantism*, Edinburgh: Oliver and Boyd, 1949.

Gosse, Philip. *The History of Piracy*. London: Green & Co., 1932.

Johnson, W. Branch. *Wolves of the Channel, 1681-1856*, London: Wishart & Co., 1931.

Pascoe, C. F. *Two Hundred Years of the S.P.G., 1701-1900. An Historical account of the Society, Based on a digest of the Society's Records*. London: n.p., 1901.

Ritchie, Carson I. A. "Papers from Lambeth Palace Library." *Catholic Record Society, Miscellanea*. London, 1964.

———. "Some Acadian Letters." *Journal of the Society of Archivists* 1, no. 4. (London, 1956).

———. *The New World*. A Catalogue of an exhibition of books, maps, manuscripts, and documents held at Lambeth Palace Library. Westminster: Church Information Board, 1957.

Ritchie, M. K. and Ritchie, C. "An Apology for the Aberdeen Evictions." *The Miscellany of the Third Spalding Club* 3 (Aberdeen, 1960).

Rowe, Henry K., *The History of Religion in the United States*. New York: Macmillan & Co., 1924.

Dictionary of National Biography, ed. Sir Leslie Stephens, London: George Smith, 1885.

Sweet, William Warren. *The Story of Religions in America*. New York and London: Harper Bros., 1930.

Index

201

DATE DUE

DATE DUE			
SEP 5 '78			
MAR 2 4 2004			
GAYLORD			PRINTED IN U.S.A.